YEMEN
in Pictures

Francesca Davis DiPiazza

Twenty-First Century Books

Contents

Lerner Publishing Group, Inc. realizes that current information and statistics quickly become out of date. To extend the usefulness of the Visual Geography Series, we developed www.vgsbooks.com, a website offering links to up-to-date information, as well as in-depth material, on a wide variety of subjects. All of the websites listed on www.vgsbooks.com have been carefully selected by researchers at Lerner Publishing Group, Inc. However, Lerner Publishing Group, Inc. is not responsible for the accuracy or suitability of the material on any website other than www.lernerbooks.com. It is recommended that students using the Internet be supervised by a parent or teacher. Links on www.vgsbooks.com will be regularly reviewed and updated as needed.

INTRODUCTION — 4

THE LAND — 8

▶ Topography. Climate. Flora and Fauna. Natural Resources. Environmental Issues. Cities.

HISTORY AND GOVERNMENT — 20

▶ Ancient Kingdoms. Trading Routes. The Spread of Religions. Yemeni Kingdoms. Foreign Invasions. Two Yemens. North Yemen. South Yemen. Republican Victory and the PDRY. Islamists and Unification. Democracy and Terrorism. Government.

THE PEOPLE — 38

▶ Health. Education. Language. Housing. Ethnic Groups and Social Structure. Status of Women.

Twenty-First Century Books
A division of Lerner Publishing Group, Inc.
241 First Avenue North
Minneapolis, MN 55401 U.S.A.

Website address: www.lernerbooks.c[...]

web enhanced @ www.vgsbooks.com

CULTURAL LIFE   46

▶ Religion. Holidays. Weddings. Music and Dance. Literature. Arts. Sports. Food.

THE ECONOMY   56

▶ Industry, Oil, and Mining. Transportation and Communications. Services and Tourism. Agriculture and Fishing. The Future.

FOR MORE INFORMATION

▶ Timeline   66
▶ Fast Facts   68
▶ Currency   68
▶ Flag   69
▶ National Anthem   69
▶ Famous People   70
▶ Sights to See   72
▶ Glossary   73
▶ Selected Bibliography   74
▶ Further Reading and Websites   76
▶ Index   78

Library of Congress Cataloging-in-Publication Data

DiPiazza, Francesca Davis.
    Yemen in pictures / by Francesca Davis DiPiazza.
        p.   cm. — (Visual geography series)
    Includes bibliographical references and index.
    ISBN 978-0-8225-7149-0 (lib. bdg. : alk. paper)
    1. Yemen—Pictorial works. I. Title.
DS247.Y42D55 2008
953.3—dc22   2006037584

Manufactured in the United States of America
1 2 3 4 5 6 – PA – 13 12 11 10 09 08

INTRODUCTION

Yemen is a Middle Eastern nation, lying at the southern tip of the Arabian Peninsula. The country of 21.6 million people is one of the poorest nations in the Arab world. In ancient times, however, Yemen was known as Arabia Felix. The name means "Happy Arabia" in Latin, the language of the Roman Empire. Its wealth came from both its location on important trade routes and its trade in frankincense and myrrh. As ingredients in perfumes and incense, these fragrant substances were in high demand in the ancient world.

The kingdom of Saba, or Sheba, arose in Yemen about 1000 B.C. This farming civilization built dams and canals that brought water to crops. Sabaean families formed close-knit clans. These extended family groups fiercely protected their lands from neighboring clans. The famed queen of Sheba, mentioned in the Bible, was a legendary Sabaean ruler. Beginning in A.D. 300 Yemen's clans and kingdoms battled foreign invaders.

The history of Yemen, like that of much of the Arabian Peninsula, is tied to the religion of Islam. Yemenis consider the rise of this faith in the seventh century A.D. to be the most important event in their history. Yemeni leaders quickly adopted the faith and introduced it to their followers.

Clans rose and fell in Yemen over the next few hundred years. Isolated by vast deserts to the north, most Yemenis lived in farming villages. By 1517 the Ottoman Turks had included Yemen in their vast Islamic empire.

Yemen's location made it important to shipping nations. It borders the water passageway that links the Red Sea to the Indian Ocean. Ottoman Turks and the British Empire both had interests in Yemen. These two powers split the country into north and south regions in 1905. North Yemen and South Yemen remained divided throughout most of the twentieth century.

Both Yemens fought for and won independence in the 1960s. Years of wars and attempts to join the two halves followed. The discovery of oil along their mutual border in 1988 motivated the two Yemens to

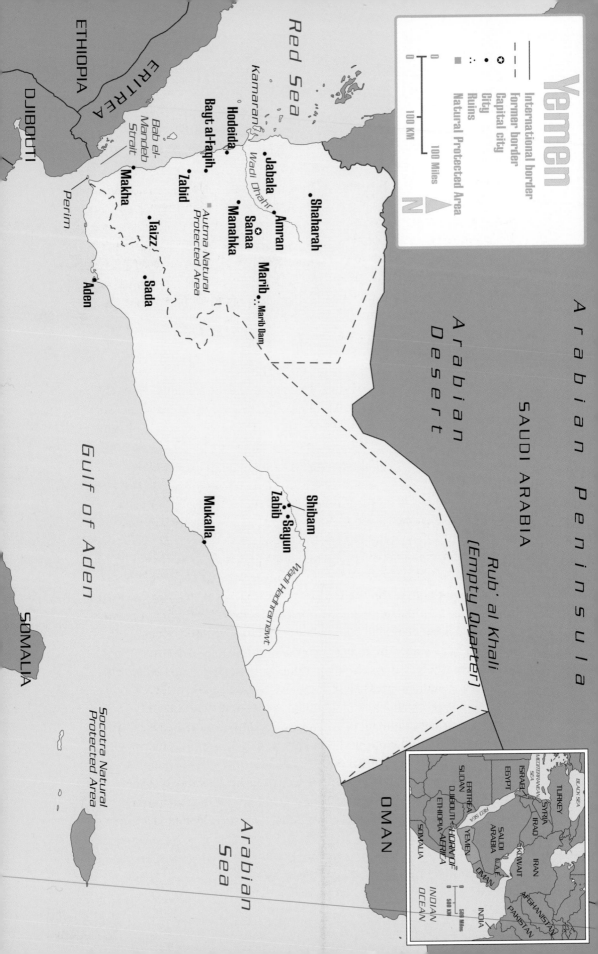

come together. In 1990 they united to form the Republic of Yemen.

At unification, Yemen worked to develop its economy while preserving its ancient culture. Many areas of the country had few schools or paved roads and little industry. Most people lived in small villages and could not read or write. The democratically elected government used money from oil to improve farming, schools, and public works.

In Arabic, Yemen's name is al-Yaman. It refers to the fact that the land lies south, or *yamanan*, of Islam's holiest city, Mecca, on the Arabian Peninsula. The entire Arabian Peninsula consists of one granite plate. The rock plate is tilted so that the southwestern edge is the highest. Because of its high position on the peninsula, one of Yemen's nicknames is the Roof of Arabia.

Political conflicts outside and inside the country affect Yemen's stability. Tension and violence between Arabs and Israelis have shaken the Middle East for decades. Yemen supports the Arab Palestinian cause against Israel, the Jewish homeland. The United States and other Western nations support Israel. Ongoing conflict in Iraq also rocks the region. Across the waters to Yemen's south lie Somalia and other East African countries damaged by civil wars. Refugees and weapons from that region flood Yemen. Within Yemen, clans sometimes clash with the government and each other, and the poorer south sometimes resents the richer north.

Tensions exploded in 2000 when terrorists in Yemen's port city of Aden bombed a U.S. ship, the USS *Cole*. Kidnappings of foreigners also brought Yemen into the international spotlight. The country gained a reputation as a dangerous place where Islamic extremists operate. Yemen's leaders work with the United States to build security. But some citizens think their government is too close to Western nations.

Yemenis hold fast to their religious and cultural heritage. Its citizens traditionally express political views through spoken poetry. Poets address issues of all sorts, including the nation's shortage of water. Water has become one of Yemen's most serious concerns. Deep wells take water from underground, but this source of water is running out.

President Ali Abdullah Saleh was reelected on September 20, 2006. He has held power in Yemen since he became president of North Yemen in 1978. Though his government has overseen some economic growth and has kept the nation fairly stable, Yemen faces many challenges.

THE LAND

Yemen is a country of mountains, plains, deserts, and islands in south-western Asia. Its 203,849 square miles (527,969 square kilometers) cover the southwest corner of the Arabian Peninsula. The country is slightly smaller than Texas. Yemen's more than one hundred islands include Socotra Island in the Gulf of Aden and the Kamaran and Perim islands in the Red Sea.

Yemen's neighbors are Oman to the east and Saudi Arabia to the north. The Red Sea forms Yemen's western border. The waters of the Gulf of Aden—part of the Indian Ocean—lap against Yemen's southern coast. The Bab el-Mandeb Strait is a narrow water passage joining the gulf and the sea. The sea and the gulf separate Yemen from the Horn of Africa, less than 200 miles (321 km) away. Across these waters, the East African countries of Eritrea and Djibouti lie to the west and Somalia to the south.

○ Topography

The topography, or landscape, of Yemen varies from rocky seacoasts to green plains to barren desert. The country's land is highest in the west. It gradually declines to low points in the east. Mountains surround the fertile highlands in the west, where most Yemenis live. The highlands slope downward to the east, into the edge of the Arabian Desert, the second-largest desert in the world. (Only the Sahara is bigger.) The desert dominates eastern Yemen. Narrow coastal plains run along Yemen's seacoasts. Six regions comprise Yemen's landscape.

Yemen's west coast is called the Tihama, meaning "hot lands" in Arabic, Yemen's official language. This flat region runs from the southern tip of Yemen north along the Red Sea into Saudi Arabia. It is a sandy coastal plain that varies between 15 and 40 miles (24 and 64 km) in width. Irrigation, or artificial watering systems, allows some farming on the coast. However, few people live in this hot area. Inland, the plain ends abruptly at a series of rocky cliffs. Over time, rain has worn away these cliffs and formed deep wadis—dry riverbeds that fill with seasonal rains.

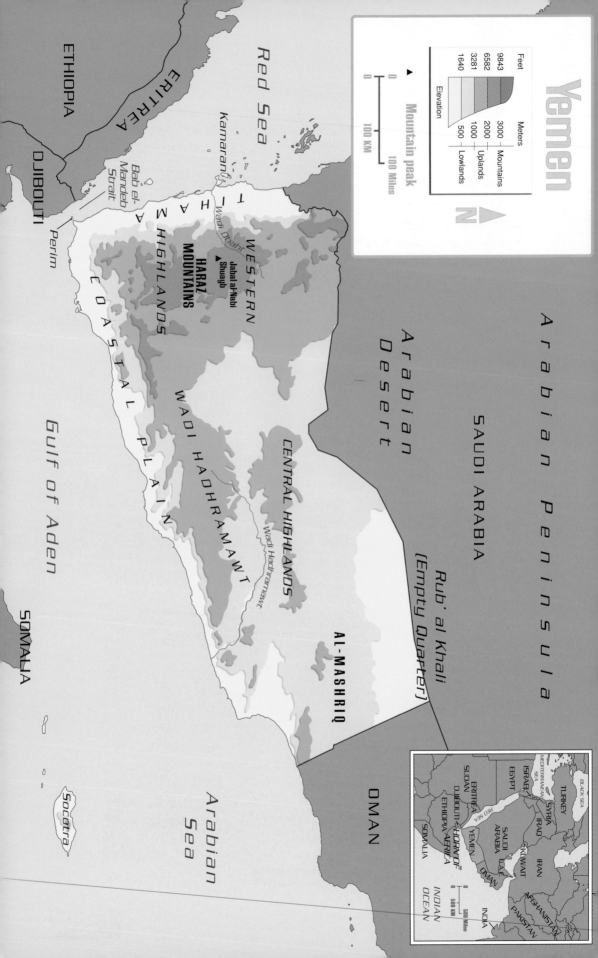

The steep mountains of the Western Highlands region rise sharply from the coastal cliffs. The mountain range stretches north to south. Many of its peaks reach more than 12,000 feet (3,700 meters) above sea level. At a height of 12,336 feet (3,760 m), Jabal al-Nabi Shuayb is the highest point on the Arabian Peninsula. Some of the mountains are volcanoes.

The Western Highlands level off at the fertile, high plateau called the Central Highlands region. Wadis and underground springs water this flat, elevated land. It contains Yemen's most productive farmland and is home to most of the country's people. The capital city, Sanaa, is located in the western part of the plateau. The Haraz Mountains are a volcanic region 50 miles (80 km) west of Sanaa. On the eastern edge of the Central Highlands is al-Mashriq, a lower mountain range. The rocky al-Mashriq gradually declines to the stone and sand of the Arabian Desert to the north and east. Surrounded by mountains, the Central Highlands are prone to earthquakes.

Eastern Yemen is dominated by the outskirts of the vast Arabian Desert, which extends northward into Saudi Arabia. Yemen's desert lands are the southern edge of the Rub al-Khali, also called the Empty Quarter, of the Arabian Desert. Yemen covers only part of the huge, sandy Empty Quarter, which extends over 250,000 square miles (647,500 sq. km). No one lives in the Empty Quarter, except a few herding people who graze their animals there in the spring.

South of the desert, the Wadi Hadhramawt region runs west and east for 99 miles (160 km). The wadi—the largest on the Arabian Peninsula—and its many branches bring water to a dry, hilly plateau across central east Yemen. Wadi Hadhramawt's broad upper valley has supported farming communities since at least the 800s B.C. Farther east, the wadi

Shibam, Yemen, lies along the Wadi Hadhramawt. It is a dry riverbed at times.

dwindles and narrows before turning sharply south to run to the sea. The area around the wadi's lower section is sparsely populated.

A ribbon of land forms the Coastal Plain region, along the Gulf of Aden. Only 5 to 10 miles (8 to 16 km) wide, the southern coast is mostly flat and sandy. A few patches of good soil allow some farming. In places, volcanic rocks break the flatness of the plain. On the southwest coast, the sea occupies an eroded volcano. This is the site of Yemen's port city Aden.

Climate

Yemen's climate varies with topography and elevation, or height above sea level. The country's many mountain ridges trap moisture from sea winds. Therefore the climate of Yemen's highlands is the best on the Arabian Peninsula. Warm, wet summers and cool, dry winters in the highlands give the country its nickname, the Green Land of Arabia.

The Tihama and the southern coast are hot throughout the year. Rainfall averages only 2 inches (5 centimeters) a year. Humidity is high along the coasts, however. During the summer months (May to September), temperatures along the coasts can rise to 120°F (49°C) during the day. Nighttime temperatures drop to 80°F (27°C). In the winter (November to February), coastal temperatures rarely fall below 65°F (18°C).

From May to September, moist winds—called monsoons—often blow from the Indian Ocean. The winds strike the mountains of the Western Highlands and cause air masses to rise and cool. The cooling air results in heavy rains, mostly falling on the foothills. In some years, the summer monsoons do not arrive, leading to droughts, or long dry periods.

In the Central Highlands, the weather is dry and mild. Temperatures in Sanaa average 57°F (14°C) in January and 71°F (22°C) in July. Average rainfall is 20 in. (51 cm) yearly. Rainy seasons in April and August fill the wadis with enough water to support a variety of crops. In the winter, winds blow westward from central Asia, bringing cool, dry air. January temperatures can drop below freezing at night, causing damaging frosts. Brief, heavy showers in the eastern plateau fill the wadis and enable Yemenis in this area to grow crops.

Lack of water, crop failure, and famine have threatened Yemen throughout history. In about 1820, an Ottoman sultan sent an elephant as a gift to a Muslim leader in Yemen. But he didn't have enough food to keep the animal alive. He had to give it away to the ruler of Egypt.

The summer monsoons do not reach the al-Mashriq or the Empty Quarter. As a result, rain seldom falls in these areas. The Empty Quarter may not receive any rain for years.

DRAGON BLOOD TREE

Socotra Island is home to three hundred kinds of plants that live nowhere else in the world. One of the most unusual is the Dragon Blood Tree *(Dracaena cinnabari)*, with an umbrella-like shape *(above)*. Its name comes from the tree's thick red sap, which oozes when the tree is cut. In the past, the sap added red color to varnish for violins and ink. Magicians who believed the dried sap was dried blood also used it in rituals.

Strong winter winds are common and sometimes cause sandstorms in the desert.

Flora and Fauna

Yemen's varied terrain holds a vast range of plants unique to the region. Sparse shrubs and hardy grasses grow in coastal areas. Mangrove trees grow along the seashore. Their aboveground roots can survive in salty water. Cactuses, tamarisks, and other flowering plants that can survive dry conditions also flourish in this region. Palms and small scrub trees cling to the rocky cliffs east of the Tihama.

The fertile valleys of the Western Highlands receive enough rain to nourish many tropical plants, such as acacias and ficus, or figs. Trees bearing tropical fruits—including mangoes, bananas, and papayas—thrive in the area's rich soil. Farmers have cleared much of the land to plant a shrub called qat (also spelled khat). Yemenis chew the qat leaves for the mild stimulant in them that gives the chewer a sense of well-being. Qat chewing is a social ritual in Yemen, and qat has largely replaced Yemen's former important crop, coffee.

Several kinds of fruit trees—including pear, apricot, and pomegranate—grow in the Central Highlands. Almond and walnut trees produce nuts. Spice plants also exist in this region. The wadis of the eastern plateau support date palm trees. The sap of myrrh trees is the source of valuable fragrant gums used in incense and perfume. In the Arabian Desert, only sparse shrubs and grasses survive.

The **carnivorous honey badger, or ratel,** has a combined head and body length of 29 in. (74 cm). Its tail may be up to 11 in. (28 cm) long.

Humans' hunting and farming activities in Yemen have driven large mammals such as the leopard and lynx close to extinction (dying out completely). But many kinds of animals remain. Small mammals—such as hares, foxes, and hyenas—live throughout central Yemen. Hedgehogs, porcupines, hyraxes (a type of shrew), and mongooses are less common. Arabian gazelles and honey badgers inhabit the Tihama. Honey badgers are one of the animal kingdom's fiercest hunters, despite their small size. Gelada baboons travel in groups in the mountains and highlands of the northwest.

Yemen's lands are home to many kinds of reptiles. Ninety species of lizards include geckos and chameleons. Poisonous cobras and vipers are among the country's forty types of snakes. Insect life includes mosquitoes and at least one hundred kinds of butterflies. Sea life includes sardines, mackerel, sharks, and squid.

More than three hundred types of birds thrive in Yemen. Twelve are unique to the country. These rare birds include the Yemen thrush and the Arabian woodpecker. Flamingos and seagulls dwell in coastal areas. Ravens and lammergeiers (vultures that look like giant falcons) live in the highlands. Weaverbirds build their elaborate nests in trees and on telephone poles in eastern Yemen. Many birds from Europe and Asia migrate to and from Africa. They stop in Yemen to rest and find food before continuing their journey.

Natural Resources

Oil is the country's most valuable natural resource. Geologists discovered oil in west central Yemen in the 1980s. A pipeline transports crude oil from several oil wells to Hodeida, a port on the Red Sea. Yemen also has large reserves of natural gas, another important energy source.

Limestone, kaolin (white clay), sand, and marble exist in great quantities throughout Yemen. These resources provide building and industrial materials. In addition, workers mine large supplies of rock salt on the western coast. Yemen has small deposits of coal, copper, lead, gold, and zinc.

Yemen's fertile soil in the west allows farmers to grow crops. The country's waters are also an important resource. Fishing is a major industry. And the nation's location on the Bab el-Mandeb Strait places it on one of the busiest shipping lanes in the world.

Environmental Issues

Yemen's most serious environmental challenge is its lack of freshwater. Experts describe Yemen as the most "water-stressed" country in the Middle East. The nation struggles to provide enough water for its people and farms. Deep wells draw water from aquifers (underground sources). Pumping enough water to meet the nation's needs threatens to dry up many aquifers, possibly as soon as 2025. The government is concerned with the water crisis. In response it has tried to limit qat growing, as the crop uses a lot of water but has no nutritional value. Qat chewing is so popular, however, the plan has not yet succeeded. Wealthier Middle Eastern countries build desalination plants to remove salt from seawater, creating drinkable water. Yemen cannot afford this expensive solution.

Yemen also faces deforestation, or the loss of woodlands. Wooded areas once covered Yemen's highlands. Farmers cut down most of the trees for fuel and building materials. Only a few stands of trees remain. The clearing of woodlands has

QAT AND WATER

Qat farming uses a huge amount of water in a country that needs to conserve water. An estimated 16 to 40 percent of national water goes to grow this plant, which has no nutritional value. The government wants to reduce qat cultivation. Besides being important to social rituals in Yemen, however, qat provides a livelihood for about 16 percent of Yemen's workers and their families. To replace qat production and trade, the government needs to give the workers equally well-paying work. And that is a difficult challenge in a country where unemployment is already 35 percent.

Creative solutions to Yemen's environmental issues include a solar desalination machine for personal use. People can make the desalinators locally from easily available materials. Using sunlight, a desalinator turns 1.5 gallons (6 liters) of salty or dirty water into drinkable water each day.

reduced Yemen's animal population. Deforestation also leads to soil erosion, as tree roots no longer hold the earth in place. Too many farm animals grazing also wear away soil. These factors lead to desertification, or the process of drylands turning to desert.

The government legally protects two natural areas. They are Socotra Island and the Autma district in Dhamar Governorate, about 79 miles (127 km) south of Sanaa.

Cities

Although most of Yemen's 21.6 million people live in small villages, the nation's cities are growing rapidly. Yemenis move to urban areas to find work in new industries. In the twenty-first century, more than 25 percent of Yemenis live in cities.

SANAA (population 1.6 million) is the capital of Yemen. Its beginnings are steeped in legend. According to Yemeni folktales, Shem, son of Noah, founded the city of Sanaa after surviving the biblical forty-day flood on Noah's ark.

Sanaa lies 140 miles (225 km) east of the Red Sea in a fertile area of the Central Highlands. Since the early 1990s, when about 500,000 people lived in the city, Sanaa has experienced a population explosion. Many Yemenis looking for work moved from rural areas to the capital. The city has spread in all directions, absorbing nearby villages and farmland.

The name of the capital city **Sanaa** means "fortified place."

Despite its rapid growth, Sanaa has preserved its medina—the old walled section of the city that dates to the first century A.D. Many of the city's houses there are more than four hundred years old. Rising to seven stories high, these dwellings are made of stone, brick, and mud. Residents paint ornate decorations on the houses with white plaster.

The medina's souk, or central market, is known as Souk al-Milh. Each craft or trade occupies a particular area—sometimes even a particular street—within the souk. Vendors sell a wide variety of goods, including pottery, carpets, and silver and copper items. Farmers offer vegetables, qat, fruits, and mounds of fragrant and colorful spices for sale.

The elaborate minarets, or towers, of mosques (Islamic houses of worship) rise above the markets and houses of Sanaa. The massive outer walls of the largest mosque, al-Jami al-Kabir, enclose fountains and buildings.

The growth of Sanaa has caused some wealthy residents of the medina to move to the city's outskirts. Modern recreation, shopping, and entertainment facilities are available there. Owners have divided the old dwellings into apartments, usually poorly cared for. To

preserve Sanaa's unique architecture, the United Nations (UN) funds restoration and preservation projects in the old walled city.

ADEN (population 510,000) is located in the crater of an extinct volcano on the southern coast. The city is Yemen's chief seaport and economic center. Aden became a key trading-hub during ancient times. It continues to be important to commerce and transportation in the Middle East. Foreign ships stop at the port to refuel and to load fish products, coffee, tobacco, cotton, and salt. Domestic and international flights land at the city's large airport. Modern roads lead from Aden to towns throughout the country. Aden is also a manufacturing center. Huge refineries there process oil, and factories produce cooking oil and textiles.

Aden's architecture reflects both its history and status as a modern urban settlement. Large, up-to-date structures line wide thorough-fares, while old buildings stand along winding, narrow streets. The city's population includes Arabs, Asians, Africans, and Europeans.

Aden, Yemen, has been an important seaport since ancient times.

Learn about the wildlife, geography, environmental issues, and city life of Yemen. Go to www.vgsbooks.com for links

TAIZZ (population 406,000) lies in southwestern Yemen. Compared with Sanaa or Aden, Taizz is young. It dates to the seventh century A.D., when it was a religious and administrative center. Periodically, Taizz has served as the nation's capital, most recently from 1948 to 1962. Famous for its mosques and markets, Taizz also has extensive modern neighborhoods.

HODEIDA (population 380,000) is a commercial port on the Red Sea. Builders constructed most of the city's buildings during the twentieth century. A marketplace stands in the oldest area of Hodeida. This area also contains beautiful houses with wooden balconies and plaster-decorated walls. Fishing remains an important industry in the city. Each morning, fishing fleets deliver catches of shark, red snapper, and kingfish to the local market.

MARIB (population 4,000) is located in west central Yemen. Though small, the city symbolizes the country's history. In ancient times, Marib was the capital of the kingdom of Saba. In about 500 B.C., the Sabaeans built an important dam here. Considered the most valuable archaeological site in Yemen, the ruins of the Sabaean culture attract tourists. An American company found oil near Marib in 1982, and an oil refinery soon opened. Marib is also a modern city of government offices, small shops, and comfortable houses.

HISTORY AND GOVERNMENT

Archaeologists, or scientists who study ancient remains, believe that the first humans came to Yemen from East Africa about forty thousand years ago. By about 5000 B.C., people in the region were using flint tools and building water channels and stone dwellings.

Separated from the rest of the Arabian Peninsula by vast deserts, Yemen was far from the large empires that rose and fell in the Middle East and North Africa. Early Yemeni merchants traded with these empires along both land and sea routes. Most ancient Yemenis, however, were farmers who grew crops for their families and clans.

Ancient Kingdoms

In about 1000 B.C., three kingdoms arose in Yemen. Saba (also called Sheba) and Qataban developed in the Central Highlands. Hadhramawt existed in eastern Yemen. At this time, the domestication of the one-humped camel was an important advance. Camels offered a range of

benefits, including transportation, meat, milk, and dung for fuel. The animals can go for weeks with no water and little food. This allowed merchants with camels to travel through harsh lands they couldn't cross before.

Each of these southern Arabian kingdoms enjoyed periods of dominance and prosperity. They also shared a common culture, which included polytheism (the worship of many gods). Because the people of the ancient kingdoms did not build walls or fortifications, archaeologists believe that the early Yemenis lived in peace.

Saba, the largest and most powerful kingdom, prospered from trade and farming. An extensive irrigation system enabled the Sabaeans to grow abundant crops. The system included dams that directed runoff from occasional rains into artificial canals. Builders constructed the largest dam in about 500 B.C. near Marib, the capital of Saba. The Sabaeans worshipped the main god Almaqah. The temple of Almaqah at Marib was an important religious site.

THE QUEEN OF SHEBA

The earliest reference to Saba (or Sheba) is in the First Book of Kings in the Hebrew Bible, or the Old Testament. The story also appears in the Quran, the holy book of Islam. While historians debate its accuracy, the story shows that Saba engaged in far-flung trade at an early date. It describes the queen of Sheba's tenth century B.C. visit to King Solomon of Jerusalem, who was famous for his wisdom:

"The queen of Sheba heard of Solomon's fame and came to test him with difficult questions. She arrived in Jerusalem with . . . camels laden with spices and an immense quantity of gold and precious stones. Having reached Solomon, she discussed with him everything that she had in mind, and Solomon had an answer for all her questions. . . . When the queen of Sheba saw how very wise Solomon was . . . it left her breathless. . . . No such wealth of spices ever came again as those which the queen of Sheba gave to king Solomon." (1 Kings 10:1–10)

The queen of Sheba *(left)* bows slightly to King Solomon *(right)*. This drawing of their meeting was made in the A.D. 1800s.

◉ Trading Routes

The early traders of southern Arabia controlled an important network of overland trails. The trade routes started in southern and western Arabia. They crossed the Arabian Peninsula to Babylonia and Mesopotamia (both in modern Iraq), Egypt, Palestine (modern Israel), and Syria.

Yemen's early kingdoms grew wealthy from the trade of frankincense and myrrh. These fragrant resins come from trees that grow only in eastern Yemen, southern Oman, and northern Africa. Ancient peoples made perfumes, medicines, and incense from the resins. Many religious ceremonies included offering the spicy smoke of burning incense to the gods. In addition to these exports, Yemeni traders sold spices, textiles, and swords from India. Silks from China and gold, ivory, and slaves from Africa also brought great wealth. Believing that all these valuable goods originated in southern Arabia, merchants from the north called Yemen Arabia Felix (Happy Arabia).

Use of the overland trails declined in the first century A.D. At that time, a Mediterranean sailor named Hippalus discovered a sea route from Egypt to India. He found that the summer monsoons could blow ships down the Red Sea, around the Arabian Peninsula, and east to India. Winter monsoons could bring ships back along the same course.

The newly discovered sea-lanes contributed to the rise of Himyar. This kingdom in the highlands held land along the Bab el-Mandeb Strait. By A.D. 50, the Himyarites had conquered southwestern Arabia and had taken charge of shipping through the strait.

Meanwhile, the Romans, based on the Italian Peninsula, had created an enormous empire. It stretched from northern Europe into North Africa. In 323 the Roman emperor Constantine made Christianity the official religion of his empire. Because the use of incense was not central to Christianity, trade of frankincense and myrrh declined. The kingdoms of southern Arabia lost much of their wealth. Following the end of Yemen's prosperity, generations of religious and political groups fought among themselves. In the coming centuries, they would also fight against outsiders who sought to control their land.

The Spread of Religions

With the rise of Christianity, missionaries, or religious teachers, entered Yemen. In the fourth and fifth centuries, Christian and Jewish missionaries arrived. Both groups were successful in converting the inhabitants of southern Arabia to their religions. Many Himyarite leaders also accepted these monotheistic (one-god) faiths.

In the early 500s, the Sabaean king Yusuf Ashaar Dhu Nuwas ordered all Christians in his realm to convert to Judaism (the Jewish religion). More than twenty thousand Christians refused and were executed. In response, the Christian king of Ethiopia, Abraha of Axum, seized Yemen in 525.

The writing on this stone is Himyaritic. It was the language of Himyar, a first century A.D. Yemeni kingdom. The stone is located near the Marib Dam.

THE RAT AND THE DAM

The Marib Dam was one of the great engineering feats of the ancient world. The dam measured 2,231 feet (680 m) long and 59 feet (18 m) high. Sabaean kings ordered it built in the sixth century B.C. It made an area of 25,000 acres (10,000 hectares) fertile. Often repaired, the dam collapsed beyond repair in A.D. 570. The Quran even records the event. This holy book declares that God was punishing the people for not giving proper thanks to him. But popular Yemeni legend says that a rat digging through the dam's walls caused its final destruction.

Under Abraha, workers tried to repair the Marib Dam, which had begun to fall apart. Despite these efforts, floods in 570 destroyed the dam, forcing many Yemeni farmers to leave southern Arabia. In the same year, Abraha and his army mounted elephants to attack the kingdoms of northern Arabia. Abraha's attempt to conquer this region failed, and the king died soon afterward. The Himyarites then asked the emperor of Persia (modern Iran) to help them get rid of the Ethiopians. In 575 the Persians defeated the Ethiopians and brought Yemeni kingdoms under Persian rule.

A new religion—Islam—soon transformed the Arabian Peninsula. A merchant named Muhammad (570–632) lived in Mecca, Saudi Arabia. About 610 he came to believe that Allah ("God" in Arabic) had chosen him as his prophet, or spiritual spokesperson. The divine messages he received form the Quran, the holy book of Islam. It offers political as well as spiritual guidance. In 628 the Persian governor of Yemen accepted Islam. The new faith spread quickly. Many Yemeni sheikhs (local leaders) converted and introduced the religion to their people. Muhammad's missionaries arrived in Yemen, and by the early 630s, workers had built the first Yemeni mosques in Sanaa.

After the death of Muhammad in 632, Muslims (followers of Islam) divided into two sects. Sunni Muslims elected their own caliph, or political and religious leader. Shiite Muslims believed that the head of Islam should be a descendant of Muhammad's daughter Fatima and her husband, Ali. The Sunnis eventually became the dominant group.

To expand Islamic territory, the first caliph, Abu Bakr, led Muslim warriors in the conquest of the Middle East and North Africa. More than twenty thousand Yemeni soldiers joined the victorious Muslim armies. Caliphs created an empire stretching from Spain through India.

The empire did not last long as a political unit. But Islam united Muslims in a shared faith, no matter where they lived. And Islamic law (sharia) gave Muslims a common guide for daily social life—

though interpretations of laws differed widely. The spread of Islam also introduced the Arabic language to many peoples.

Yemeni Kingdoms

In 661 the Umayyad dynasty (family of rulers) took over the caliphate. They moved their capital from Mecca to Damascus (in present-day Syria), but Islam's religious center remained in Mecca. Yemen became a province of the Umayyad Empire. When the Abbasid clan seized power from the Umayyads in 715, they established their capital in Baghdad (in present-day Iraq). Yemen's distance from Islam's political and cultural hubs allowed several small, nearly independent kingdoms to develop in southern Arabia.

THE ZIYADIDS Dissatisfied with Abbasid rule, two groups in the Tihama region rebelled in 819. The caliph in Baghdad sent Muhammad ibn Ziyad to restore order. After putting down the revolt, ibn Ziyad founded the independent realm of Zabid, which lasted several hundred years. Ibn Ziyad used the important al-Ashair Mosque in Zabid as a university. Scholars there studied Islam, mathematics, history, and poetry.

THE ZAYDIS In 892 the caliph sent a descendant of Muhammad, Yahya al-Rassi, to settle a war between two rival clans in northwestern Yemen. In 897 al-Rassi became the first imam—the political land religious leader of the Muslim community—of the Zaydi dynasty. This ruling family would last almost one thousand years, longer than any other Yemeni dynasty.

The Zaydis were Muslims of the Shiite branch of Islam. Their beliefs were similar to the Sunnis', but all their imams had to be kin of the prophet Muhammad. Zaydi rule was organized around many different clans. The loyalty of each clan to the imam was more sacred than bonds with other Muslims. The study of war was also very important. Expertise in war enabled the Zaydis to survive centuries of attacks and to rise to power again and again.

> No matter which group they belonged to, Yemenis looked to their leaders to follow the Quran's command to "enjoin [order] the good and forbid the evil."

THE SULAYHIDS In 1046 Ali al-Sulayhi founded the Sulayhid state in Sanaa. Al-Sulayhi was a follower of the Ismaili faith—a branch of Shiite Islam. For the next seventeen years, the Sulayhids fought with other sects. Al-Sulayhi's army conquered his opponents and united the Yemeni kingdoms under his rule in 1063.

In 1067 al-Sulayhi's son and successor died. Queen Arwa, the son's wife, inherited the throne. A popular ruler, she was called *al-sayyida al-hurra*, Arabic for "the noble lady who is free and independent." She tried to establish clan loyalty through fair administration. Arwa died in 1138. With no heirs to the throne, the Sulayhid dynasty ended.

THE AYYUBIDS AND THE RASULIDS In 1173 the Ayyubid rulers from Egypt conquered Yemen. They made it a self-governing state within the Ayyubid Empire. Unable to rule a remote area like Yemen effectively, the Ayyubids left control in the hands of a local official named Nur al-Din Umar ibn al-Rasul. He proclaimed Yemen an independent nation. Centered in Taizz, the Rasulid family ruled from 1228 to 1454.

Foreign Invasions

By the early 1500s, Europeans—including Portuguese merchants—were using the sea route between Egypt and India for trade and conquest. In 1507 the Portuguese annexed (took over) the island of Socotra in the Indian Ocean. From Socotra, they tried to seize Yemen. In 1513 the Portuguese adventurer Afonso de Albuquerque led an unsuccessful invasion of Aden. To protect its interests in the Red Sea, Egypt sent a large fleet to Yemen. The Egyptians captured the Tihama and the highlands around Sanaa. Egypt's attack on Aden, however, failed.

In 1517 armies of the Ottoman Empire (based in modern Turkey) conquered Egypt. By 1548 the Ottoman Turks had brought most of

This seventeenth-century drawing portrays the port city of Aden, Yemen.

Yemen under their control. They would hold power off and on in various ways in Yemen for almost four hundred years. Under Ottoman rule, Yemenis harvested coffee beans from the highlands and developed an extensive coffee trade. Makha, a port on the Red Sea, became the most important coffee port in the world.

In 1590 Qasim the Great, a young descendant of the Zaydi imams, began a resistance movement against the Ottoman Turks. Qasim attracted Yemenis from throughout the region to his cause. Shiites and Sunnis united for the first time, and they elected Qasim imam. By 1608 he had gathered enough support to force the Turks into a ten-year truce. According to the terms of the agreement, Qasim controlled his provinces, and the Ottomans handled foreign affairs. Turkish occupation ended in 1636, when Yemen united under the leadership of Qasim's son Muayyad Muhammad.

Under the Zaydis, centralized control of Yemen fell apart as some groups proclaimed their independence. In the 1700s, the expanding British Empire also threatened Zaydi rule. The British wanted to establish a commercial port in southern Arabia to supply their colony in India. In 1799 the British seized the island of Perim near the Bab el-Mandeb Strait. In 1839 they conquered Aden.

In 1849 the Ottoman Turks returned to Yemen and occupied the Tihama. Twenty years later, the Suez Canal opened. This artificial waterway connects the Mediterranean Sea and the Red Sea. It shortens the distance between Great Britain and India by 5,000 miles (8,047 km). The canal made Yemen even more important to the British. Their ships sailed through the canal and stopped at Aden for supplies on their way to India.

By 1882 the Turks had taken control of much of northwestern Yemen, including Sada, the Zaydi capital. The Turkish expansion alarmed the British, who controlled much of southern Yemen. To protect their trade routes, the British signed treaties with many Yemeni sheikhs. These clan leaders agreed that they would not sell or give away any territory without British approval. They would also notify British officials if any foreigners attempted to interfere with the sheikhs' affairs. In exchange, the British promised military protection.

Between 1901 and 1905, the Turks and the British drew the border between their two territories. The Turkish territory became North Yemen. The British territory became South Yemen. The boundary was recognized both locally and internationally. It would remain intact for most of the twentieth century.

The Turks' occupation of North Yemen did not go unchallenged,

THE ZAYDIS' CLAIM

In 1906 the Zaydi imam Yahya challenged the right of outsiders to rule Yemen. Yahya wrote, "The land of Yemen was in the hands of our ancestors, the most noble family [of the Prophet Muhammad], from the [ninth century A.D.] to the present. . . . There were constant battles between our ancestors and those who opposed them, thus opposing the wish of the people of Yemen to be ruled by their lords and the sons of their Prophet. . . ."

—quoted in Dresch, *History of Modern Yemen*, p. 6.

however. Throughout the early 1900s, the Zaydis—along with several northern Tihama groups led by Sayyid Muhammad al-Idrisi—staged many uprisings. In 1911, to end the fighting, the Zaydis and the Turks signed the Treaty of Daan. The treaty gave the Zaydis rule over northern Yemen.

◉ Two Yemens

The Ottoman Empire collapsed after its defeat in World War I (1914–1918). The war had pitted the Turks and Germany against Britain, France, and Russia. North Yemen became fully independent of the Ottomans in 1918. The Zaydi ruler, Imam Yahya, continued his reign. South Yemen remained under British control.

The British divided South Yemen into three parts—a colony and two protectorates (regions dependent on a foreign government). The Aden Colony surrounded and included the port city of Aden. The Western Protectorate contained the southern third of the Central Highlands and al-Mashriq. It stretched from the tip of the Arabian Peninsula east to the Wadi Hadhramawt. The Eastern Protectorate included all of present-day eastern Yemen.

Britain ruled the protectorates through local leaders. The British intervened only in cases of internal power struggles and border disputes with North Yemen. In the Aden Colony, Yemenis eager for self-government expressed discontent with British control through frequent strikes. Despite the unrest, Aden and some parts of the protectorates experienced growth and modernization.

The British also showed interest in expanding their territory to include North Yemen. Imam Yahya had secured his power in North Yemen by isolating his people from outside influences. Yahya refused any attempts to negotiate. As a result, the British allowed opponents of the Zaydis to use Aden as a base. In 1948 a member of one of these opposition groups assassinated the imam.

Yahya's son Ahmad changed his father's policy by accepting foreign aid. He formed diplomatic ties with Britain, the United States, and the

OPERATION MAGIC CARPET

Israel was created as a Jewish homeland in 1948, replacing the Arab state of Palestine. In protest, Muslims in Aden destroyed Yemeni Jews' homes and stores. Rioters killed eighty-two people. The following year, British and American planes made almost 380 flights in a secret operation called Operation Magic Carpet. They flew almost all of Yemen's forty-nine thousand Jews—many of whom had never seen a plane before—to resettle in Israel.

In the late 1940s, Jewish refugees *(above)* from Aden Colony and the two Yemen protectorates wait to be admitted to a refugee camp in Israel.

Soviet Union. (The Soviet Union was a country from 1922 to 1991, whose territory included Russia.) Ahmad also allowed foreign countries to explore for oil. Despite Ahmad's efforts to open North Yemen to the rest of the world, the region itself made little progress. By the end of Ahmad's reign in 1962, North Yemen still had poor roads, no schools, few doctors, and no manufacturing facilities.

North Yemen

Imam Ahmad's death brought his son Muhammad al-Badr to power. One week into Imam Muhammad's reign, Colonel Abdullah al-Sallal led a group of army officers in a coup. They overthrew the Zaydi dynasty and formed a republic. The new regime named the country the Yemen Arab Republic (YAR), known as North Yemen. Al-Sallal became its prime minister.

Most Arab countries welcomed the new nation. But Saudi Arabia and Jordan did not. These monarchies had supported the dynastic rule of North Yemen. After al-Sallal's revolt, North Yemen became a member of the United Nations.

Imam Muhammad fled to the northern mountains. There his uncle was organizing an opposition force called the royalists. Britain and Saudi Arabia supported the royalists. Civil war broke out in 1962, when the royalists clashed with al-Sallal's republican army. Egypt and the Soviet Union supported the republicans. Both nations wanted to ally themselves with North Yemen. Fierce fighting caused many casualties on both sides.

South Yemen

In South Yemen, violence also erupted during the 1960s. The British had established the Federation of South Arabia to unite the protectorates with the Aden Colony. But residents of Aden who wanted independence for the colony opposed this action. Britain's promise that it would eventually grant independence to the federation did not halt the violence.

A rebel movement quickly formed the National Liberation Front (NLF). In 1963 the nationalists staged an uprising, and warfare broke out in and near Aden. By 1967 the NLF had forced the British to withdraw from South Yemen. The land officially gained its independence in November 1967. The NLF declared the founding of the People's Republic of South Yemen.

Qahtan al-Shabi became the leader of the new country. It allied itself with the Soviet Union and with other Communist nations. Communist governments strictly control their economies. The loss of British trade and investment, however, caused serious economic problems for South Yemen. Al-Shabi put some sectors of the economy under government control. In addition, South Yemen began receiving aid from the Communist countries of Eastern Europe.

Republican Victory and the PDRY

By 1967 the civil war in the north had reached a stalemate. Disputes

In Aden, Yemen, British troops arrest Yemeni demonstrators on April 4, 1967.

arose among various groups within the republican ranks. Al-Sallal and his backers believed that North Yemen would survive only if it established friendly relations with Saudi Arabia. They believed they needed the support of the oil-rich kingdom that covered most of the Arabian Peninsula. This view was unpopular among many republicans because Saudi Arabia was helping the royalists. In late 1967, these anti-Saudi factions replaced al-Sallal with Abd al-Rahman al-Iryani.

The Soviet Union and groups opposed to British rule in South Yemen supported al-Iryani's new government. The government, therefore, was able to hold back the royalists. The republicans also persuaded Saudi Arabia to end support for the royalist cause.

South Yemen formed even closer ties to the Communist countries in 1969, when Salim Rubay Ali overthrew al-Shabi. Strongly pro-Communist, Rubay Ali changed the name of the country to the People's Democratic Republic of Yemen (PDRY), known as South Yemen.

In 1970, after more than 200,000 North Yemenis had been killed, the war ended with a republican victory. The government sent Imam Muhammad into exile in Iraq, ending Zaydi rule. In July 1970, Saudi Arabia formed diplomatic ties with North Yemen.

By the early 1970s, the two independent Yemeni states had restructured their governments. But both countries faced the enormous task of rebuilding their economies. Many years of conflict had damaged both economies. To accomplish this goal, both nations had to rely on foreign aid. North Yemen received most of its money from Saudi Arabia and European countries. South Yemen obtained funds from the Soviet Union. Because the Saudis and the Soviets were hostile to one another, the two Yemens were also at odds.

This conflict led to border fighting between North Yemen and South Yemen in the early 1970s. Negotiations stopped the fighting in October 1972, when the two Yemens agreed to merge within a year. The merger was postponed because the prime ministers of both countries were unable to persuade their political leaders to accept the plan. Border skirmishes began again. Relations between the two countries grew worse.

North Yemen changed leadership many times during the rest of the 1970s. In 1974 a member of the government overthrew al-Iryani. Unknown assassins murdered two of al-Iryani's successors. North Yemen accused South Yemen of plotting the second assassination. As a result, the two Yemens clashed briefly. After the fighting ended, leaders of the two nations signed another agreement to unify.

Islamists and Unification

Two international events in 1979 would have long-lasting effects in the Muslim world, including Yemen. That year, Islamists—Muslims

ISLAMIST MILITANTS

Islam is a political and social system as well as a spiritual one. Sharia (Islamic law) rules all aspects of society, from diet to crime. *Islamist* is a word used for people who believe sharia should govern a country's private and public life. *Islamic fundamentalist* is a related term. Fundamentalists of any religion want strict obedience of the core values they believe in. Extremist Islamist militants are willing to use violence for their cause of political Islam. Al-Qaeda is an international network of Islamist militants. It has declared jihad (holy war) on Americans, Jews, and their allies. Experts suspect that al-Qaeda has bases in Yemen.

who want religious law to govern their countries—led the Islamic Revolution against the secular (non-religious) government of Iran. Their success in creating an Islamic nation inspired Islamists around the world.

In late 1979, Soviet troops began an occupation of Afghanistan, which would last ten years. The Soviet Union wanted to keep Afghanistan's pro-Communist government in power. Troops from Yemen joined Afghani rebels who wanted an Islamic government. The anti-Communist United States ran camps to train and support these and other Muslim fighters in Afghanistan. Among the Muslims was a wealthy man named Osama bin Laden. Originally from Saudi Arabia, bin Laden started a network called al-Qaeda—meaning "the base" in Arabic. The network helped organize large numbers of Muslims to fight the Afghan war against the Soviets.

During the 1980s, North Yemen, led by President Ali Abdullah Saleh, steadily improved its economy and its relations with other countries. South Yemen, on the other hand, struggled with political turmoil and economic hard times. In 1986 a civil war between two political groups in Aden killed at least three thousand people. Economic decline in the Soviet Union caused the Soviets to reduce financial aid to South Yemen.

The two Yemens moved closer to unification in the mid-1980s. Their motivation was the recently found oil deposits in the northern desert bordering both nations. Instead of dividing the oil fields, the governments shared the area.

In November 1989, Yemeni leaders agreed on a timetable for merging the two countries. The legislatures of both countries approved a new constitution in May 1990. On May 22, the Republic of Yemen was established. The two countries became one, creating the first multiparty democracy on the Arabian Peninsula.

Although tensions existed among Yemeni clans, political parties, and religious groups, most citizens welcomed unification. Yemenis took to the streets in celebration. Government officials rolled away the concrete-

At the **Yemen unification ceremony on May 22, 1990,** President Ali Abdullah Saleh, leader of the former North Yemen *(left)*, and vice president Ali Salim al-Baid, leader of the former South Yemen *(right)*, link hands.

filled barrels that had marked checkpoints on the borders between north and south. The first national elections were scheduled for thirty months later. During this time, the new government planned to finalize the nation's legal and administrative structure.

At the time of unification, North Yemen had a population of about 11 million. It was not a rich country, but its people usually had enough to eat. Its leader, Saleh, became the president of the united country. Only about 2.5 million people lived in much poorer South Yemen. Ali Salim al-Baid from South Yemen became the new vice president. Sanaa became the political capital and Aden the economic capital.

At unification, Yemen struggled to develop its economy. The nation depended on trade and aid from Iraq, Saudi Arabia, and Kuwait. In August 1990, Iraq's invasion of Kuwait put some of this aid at risk. The invasion led to the first Persian Gulf War in early 1991 between Iraq and U.S.-led international forces based in Saudi Arabia.

Yemen opposed the action that quickly drove Iraq out of Kuwait. Yemen wanted an Arab solution to the war, without Western involvement. In response, the Saudis sent more than 700,000 Yemeni workers in Saudi Arabia back to Yemen. Their return caused severe unemployment and economic hardship. The workers had been sending money back to Yemen. Its loss hit many

Two major political parties competed in the first elections in unified Yemen. Both claimed they would run the state based on "system and law"—or *wa-l-qanun* in Arabic. Yemenis who didn't trust the promises of politicians changed *wa-l-qanun* to *wa-l-salun,* meaning the politicians favored "fancy cars."

families hard. Support for Iraq remained high among Yemen's people. However, the government did not want to alienate Western nations. In addition, refugees from the war-torn African nation of Somalia were entering the country, putting a further strain on Yemen's economy.

By this time, the Soviets had withdrawn from Afghanistan, and a strict Islamist government called the Taliban had come to power there. Osama bin Laden was organizing and financing terrorist attacks on Western targets, such as embassies around the world. Other militant Islamists joined bin Laden and al-Qaeda. They included some Yemenis willing to take up arms. In general, the Islamists resented the support of Israel by Western nations, including Great Britain and the United States. They also considered Western culture immoral and materialistic. They wished to reform society by adopting traditional Islamic ways of life.

Democracy and Terrorism

Unified Yemen's economy slowly grew. Financial aid from other countries helped stabilize the country. Yemen's first national elections occurred in 1993. Voters elected a government made up of ruling parties from both the north and south.

One year later, Yemen again experienced civil war. Vice President al-Baid claimed that the national government favored the richer and more powerful north over the south. He moved to Aden and declared the south independent in May 1994. President Saleh declared a state of emergency. Fighting broke out and killed thousands of people and destroyed property. Saleh's forces triumphed in July. Al-Baid and his supporters fled abroad.

Yemen remained one nation, but the many different groups within society were not unified. Yemen's government struggled to control the unruly country in an unstable region. Furthermore, the empty desert along Yemen's borders allowed people and weapons to cross easily. These open borders continue to make the country vulnerable to terrorism.

In 1997 two Yemeni citizens claimed the planet Mars for Yemen. They demanded that the United States stop landing spacecraft on Mars until they asked for written permission. The government of Yemen stated officially that the men were abnormal.

In early 1999, a small extremist group kidnapped sixteen foreign tourists. Four of the hostages died during the attempt to free them. Yemeni courts sentenced three kidnappers to death, including the group's leader. Also that year, Yemenis participated in the first election to directly elect their president. They elected Saleh, who had been serving as president since unification.

In the summer of 2000, Yemen settled a fifty-year-old border dispute with its powerful neighbor Saudi Arabia. But peace between neighbors was far from the case throughout the Middle East. Violence between Israelis and Palestinians led to mounting Arab anger against the United States and its allies for their support of Israel. Officially, Yemen supported Palestinian resistance to Israel and the creation of an independent Palestinian state.

On October 12, 2000, the U.S. naval vessel USS *Cole* was refueling in the port of Aden. Bombers blew up a small boat next to the ship, killing themselves and seventeen U.S. sailors. Yemen's government arrested Islamist militants in connection with the attack. The United States believed Osama bin Laden had helped plan the attack. That same month, four Yemenis exploded a bomb at the British embassy in Yemen. The aim of the attacks on Western targets was to drive Western political and military interests away from the Middle East. The United States stopped using the port at Aden for refueling, due to security risks. Terrorists aided by al-Qaeda struck the United States directly on September 11, 2001. The United States and its allies invaded Afghanistan soon afterward. They claimed that the Islamic government there, the Taliban, had helped al-Qaeda. They also suspected militants from Yemen had been involved. Many Yemenis had ties with Afghanis from the 1980s, when they fought together against the Soviets. The leadership of Yemen did not want antigovernment action by Islamists in their country. They did want Yemen to continue to receive aid from Western nations. President Saleh met with President George W. Bush in the United States. Saleh pledged Yemen as a partner in the fight against global terrorism.

The bombing of the USS *Cole* on October 12, 2000, blew a big hole in its hull *(left)*.

Officials in Yemen feared that their country was becoming a safe haven for Islamist extremists. They arrested or deported (sent away) hundreds of suspected al-Qaeda members. In the fall of 2002, however, terrorists badly damaged the French supertanker *Limburg*, carrying oil off Yemen's coast. Again officials believed al-Qaeda was responsible.

Various groups in Yemen called for their government to stop cooperating with the United States because of its support of Israel. Nevertheless, President Saleh worked closely with the United States. His government allowed teams of U.S. military experts into Yemen to help with counterterrorism training. Though the two governments did not agree on all matters, they worked together toward the goal of peace and stability in Yemen.

In April 2003, a U.S.-led force invaded Iraq and removed the regime of Saddam Hussein. Anti-Western feeling increased in Yemen. Protestors publicly burned U.S. and Israeli flags.

The next year, hundreds of representatives from sixty countries attended a meeting in Yemen on democracy and human rights. President Saleh's government issued the Sanaa Declaration afterward. It stressed the importance of political and social freedoms. Saleh said that democracy was the right choice for all people, but that change must come from within societies. He stated that democracy cannot be imposed from outside, as the United States was trying to do in Iraq. Tension between the United States and Yemen flared.

Meanwhile, Yemen faced its own internal conflicts. Analysts suggest that the government's failure to meet the basic needs of its citizens led to increased support for extremism. In 2004 President Saleh accused a northern Shiite sect called the Young Believers of trying to overthrow his government and impose religious law. Clashes between government forces and the rebels led to hundreds of deaths in 2005, making it the bloodiest internal conflict since the 1994 civil war. Rebel leaders agreed to end the struggle in return for a legal pardon. Nature took its toll on the country that year when a landslide destroyed a village near Sanaa, killing more than sixty people.

President Saleh met with President Bush in the United States again in 2005. The two countries are important partners in counterterrorism efforts. In September 2006, Yemenis reelected Saleh in a landslide. Though this is only his second official term, Saleh has held power since 1978, when he became president of North Yemen. The mostly

Learn more about the ancient and modern history of Yemen and its government. Go to www.vgsbooks.com for links.

fair and peaceful elections sent a signal to the world that democracy is working in this Islamic country. Yemen's government relies on good relations and aid from other nations to win the battle against al-Qaeda.

Besides tensions in the Middle East, long-running conflicts across the Gulf of Aden in Africa also threatens Yemen's security. Almost twenty-three thousand Somali refugees arrived in Yemen in late 2006. Fleeing renewed fighting between Islamists and warlords in their country, they joined the sixty thousand already in Yemen. Security forces in Yemen arrested eight men trying to smuggle weapons from Yemen to Somalia's Islamist fighters.

In 2007 the northern Young Believers again clashed with government forces, leading to dozens of deaths. The rebels claim a complex mix of complaints against the government, including discrimination against their Shiite minority. They also object to Yemen working closely with the West. Some international observers fear that these and many other divisions in Yemen could tear the country apart, as warring factions have torn Somalia apart.

⊙ Government

The 1990 constitution that joined North Yemen and South Yemen recognizes Islam as Yemen's official religion and Arabic as its official language. Yemen's constitution provides for a multiparty democracy. Changes to the constitution in 2001 expanded the president's powers. All citizens eighteen years and older are eligible to vote.

The president heads Yemen's executive branch. The people elect the president to a seven-year term, with a limit of two terms. The president appoints a vice president and chooses cabinet members to advise the government. The president also appoints the prime minister.

The legislative branch is composed of a bicameral (two-house) parliament. Citizens elect 301 legislators to six-year terms in the House of Representatives. The president appoints 111 members to the Shura Council. (*Shura* means "consultation.")

Yemen's independent judicial branch is made up of a high council that oversees administrative matters and a Supreme Court that decides the constitutionality of laws. In addition, the government established 270 primary courts and 13 courts of appeal. The legal system is based on Islamic law, Turkish law, English law, and local customary law. As an Islamic state, Yemen's laws are not allowed to contradict the Quran.

The president appoints governors to oversee Yemen's nineteen governates. The capital of Sanaa forms its own administrative district. Governates are further divided into districts. District councils, elected by the local people, govern these smaller divisions. The president appoints mayors to run the cities.

THE PEOPLE

Unlike other peoples of the Arabian Peninsula, Yemen's people have mostly lived as settled farmers and traders, not wandering nomads. Most modern Yemenis still live on farms and in small villages scattered across the country. After the unification of the two Yemens, many people moved to cities in search of jobs. Nearly 26 percent of Yemen's 21.6 million people live in cities. Yemen's population density is among the lowest in the Middle East, with only 106 people per square mile (41 people per sq. km).

However, those numbers are growing quickly. Yemen's population ranks as the fifteenth fastest-growing population in the world. The average Yemeni woman gives birth six times in her lifetime. The nation also has one of the youngest populations in the world—about 46 percent are age 14 or under. The large number of young women reaching childbearing age guarantees the population will continue to grow. Experts expect the population to reach 38.8 million people by 2025. The government views the birth rate as too high.

One way of looking at the welfare of a nation's people is to consult the United Nations' Human Development Index. It ranks countries by comparing key areas such as health, schooling, life expectancy, and income. Lower numbers reflect higher development. The United States ranks 8 out of the 177 countries studied. Yemen ranks 150 out of 177. It is similar to its neighbors in East Africa, Djibouti (148) and Eritrea (157). Its oil-rich northern neighbor Saudi Arabia ranks 76.

◉ Health

Doctors and health care workers in Yemen are well trained. Lack of government spending, however, limits the people's access to medical care and facilities. Fewer than one hundred hospitals serve the entire country. Only 1 doctor exists per 5,000 people. Rural clinics especially struggle without enough equipment and staff.

Life expectancy at birth in Yemen is 60 years—62 for women and 59 for men. Only 4 percent of the population lives to be older than 65.

In the larger region, only Iraq's life expectancy of 59 years is lower than Yemen's. Israeli life expectancy is 80 years—the region's highest.

The government also has far to go in supplying clean, drinkable water for Yemenis. Diseases caused by polluted water—including dysentery and schistosomiasis—are common. Schistosomiasis is also called snail fever. Snails carry the larva parasites that cause the severe disease, which leads to blood loss and damaged flesh. In addition, few children receive shots against measles and other childhood diseases. Illnesses therefore spread quickly among young Yemenis. Tuberculosis, a lung disease, is another health concern for Yemenis. HIV/AIDS (human immunodeficiency virus/acquired immunodeficiency syndrome) infects 0.1 percent of the adult population.

Lack of health care and poor sanitation conditions contribute to a high mortality rate for infants and mothers. For every 1,000 live births, 75 Yemeni babies die before they reach the age of one. In comparison, the infant mortality rate of the region averages 42 deaths per 1,000 babies. Health care workers are present at only 22 percent of births in Yemen. A woman's chance of dying from childbearing-related causes is 1 in 19. Malnutrition, caused by insufficient healthy food, also threatens Yemenis' health. Without enough healthy food, many children are stunted, or do not grow big and strong.

The Yemeni government strives to provide better health care. Foreign aid has allowed some new hospitals to be built, and some rural health care programs have begun operating. A school of medicine at the University of Sanaa trains health care workers.

Education

For much of Yemen's history, formal education was available only to wealthy people. The majority of the population was illiterate, meaning they could not read or write. Girls and women especially were discouraged from schooling. Many students learned the Quran by memorizing and reciting its prayers and rules. Yemenis still highly respect the power of memory.

Yemen's centuries-old culture of spoken poetry has provided an informal kind of education, as people compose, share, and memorize poems. Poetry is a vehicle to solve problems, manage differences, and express feelings. And it offers a socially acceptable way for men and women to talk to each other.

Yemen's constitution states that all citizens have the right to an education. The law requires all children between the ages of six and fifteen to attend school. However, only 65 percent of children go to school, with far more boys than girls attending. Girls are kept home to help with the work. To encourage girls' schooling, the government has

Yemeni schoolgirls visit among themselves outside of their school in Sanaa.

removed school fees for girls. The government spends about 21 percent of its budget on education and aims to increase primary school enrollment to 85 percent.

Literacy rates have risen to 50 percent of the overall population—an improvement from preunification figures. Yemen has the biggest difference in literacy rates between men and women in the world. More than 70 percent of men are literate, while only 30 percent of women can read and write. These figures are improving among young people. Young women are 50 percent literate, and young men are 84 percent literate.

Public schools exist in large cities and towns. In many rural villages, children attend classes at Muslim religious schools. Less than half the children who attend primary school go on to high school. Universities opened in Sanaa in 1974 and in Aden in 1975. They offer courses in a variety of subjects, including history, science, math, economics, and law. Technical colleges and teacher-training institutes are located throughout the country. Literacy Through Poetry is a program that began in 2004. It seeks to teach women to read and write by documenting their own poetry and that of other women in their community.

Language

People speak Arabic, Yemen's official language, throughout the country. Arabic exists in three forms. Classical Arabic is the literary language of the Quran. This written language has not changed for hundreds of years. Modern Standard Arabic (MSA) comes from Classical Arabic. Writers in the press and in literature use MSA

COMMON ARABIC GREETINGS

"Hello" in Arabic is *marhaba* or *ahlan*. The reply is *marhabtayn* or *ahlayn*. *Ma'assalama* means "good-bye." Other common greetings are *as-salam alaykum* (peace be with you). The reply is *walaykum as-salam* (and peace to you). *Sabaah al-kair* means "good morning," and *mesah al-kair* means "good evening." "Thank-you" is *shukran*, and "you're welcome" is *afwan*.

across the Arab world. It is also the spoken language of the media—broadcasters on the all-Arab TV station al-Jazeera, for instance, speak MSA. Everyday Arabic, spoken in many different Arab nations, varies widely. Speakers of one dialect (variation) of everyday Arabic cannot always understand speakers of another. Arabic script is rounded and flowing. Its connected characters are written and read from right to left.

People of the ancient kingdom of Saba spoke non-Arabic languages. People who study languages place them among the South Semitic family of languages. Modern relatives of these languages survive in Yemen, though only about 110,000 people speak them. Some people on the island of Socotra speak Soqotri. About 70,000 people in the far east speak Mehri, and only 200 speakers of Bathari exist. These South Arabian tongues are similar to Semitic languages spoken across the Red Sea in Ethiopia and Eritrea.

Some Yemeni students also learn English. Yemenis from African and South Asian nations speak their own languages. Ethiopians, for instance, speak Amharic.

◉ Housing

Yemeni families are large, and several generations of a family often live together in a single house. Houses differ from region to region. In the coastal areas, dwellings display an African style. People make round or rectangular dwellings from mud-covered reeds and sticks. Many households consist of several one-room buildings. Each building serves a specific purpose. For example, a family might cook in one dwelling, entertain in a separate building, and sleep in yet another. Interior walls often feature painted scenes. Earthen walls or stone fences usually surround the reed homes of Tihama coastal villages.

Yemenis in the highlands build stone and clay houses that are six or seven stories high. Colored glass, carved wood, and alabaster decorate these houses. The stables and storage rooms occupy the lower levels. Several generations of one family usually share the upper levels. They contain living rooms, kitchens, bathrooms, and one large room—called a *diwan*—that is used for celebrations. The owner of the house

Traditional homes along Yemen's coast are constructed of sticks and reeds and cemented together with mud.

meets guests on the top floor, called the *mafraj*. Here men gather to chew qat and talk separately from women.

In the wadis of eastern Yemen, residents build their homes with Indian techniques. Indian architecture greatly influenced Yemen during British rule. Villagers make their houses, mosques, and public wells with sun-dried bricks. These handmade bricks decorate the buildings' outside walls.

Ethnic Groups and Social Structure

Almost all Yemenis are Arabs. Africans, mostly fleeing conflict in the Horn of Africa, have moved to Yemen. Indians and Pakistanis from South Asia also live in Yemen.

Religion, occupation, and family clan connections play large roles in the Yemeni social structure. Family and clan loyalty are of central importance. Ongoing clan rivalries trouble many parts of Yemen. The Zaydis live in northwestern Yemen. As the descendants of Muhammad and members of the Zaydi sect, the elite *sayyids* receive many privileges. For years, they have had access to advanced education and have filled administrative and legal positions. Some sayyids engage in trade and own much fertile farmland. Although the revolutions in the 1960s ended Zaydi rule, the wealthy sayyids still hold important places in Yemeni society, government, and the military.

Within a community, the leading families of each clan elect sheikhs, who belong to those families. Together the sheikhs form an important group that has the power to settle disputes in the community. Some sheikhs head large clans that can influence governmental decisions.

The *qadhi*, another elite group, are specialists in law. They fill judgeships and scholarly posts. The ancestors of this group ruled Yemeni kingdoms before the spread of Islam. *Qudha* (plural of *qadhi*) are considered educated people who have earned the respect of the community for their wisdom.

Artisans and merchants organize into guilds based on the nature of their craft. For example, the *manasib* are skilled craftspeople. Manasibs are often goldsmiths and blacksmiths. The *muzayyin*, on the other hand, hold less-skilled jobs, such as barbering, butchering, and bricklaying. The *akhdam*, who were traditionally street cleaners, are manual laborers.

After unification, the country's social structure began to change. As new economic opportunities became available, money and material goods became more important. As a result, jobs that were once considered low in status command more respect.

Go to www.vgsbooks.com for links to websites with more information about health, education, and the people of Yemen.

◎ Status of Women

Experts consider inequality between the sexes as one of the main obstacles to development in the Arab region. Unlike in conservative Saudi Arabia, Yemeni women can own property, drive cars, divorce, vote, and run for political office. In urban centers, an increasing number of Yemeni women work outside their homes. Nevertheless, Yemen has the area's greatest gap between opportunities in education, work, and politics for men and women.

Men have the final decision-making power in Yemeni families. And traditional Islamic values still restrict women in some aspects of daily life. Most Yemeni women do not eat in public restaurants, for instance. In public they usually cover themselves with robes and veils, leaving only their eyes uncovered. At home, women engage in traditional activities, such as cooking and cleaning for the family. Women and men operate separately, especially during social activities. Women meet together in the afternoons. At these *tafritas*, or gatherings, women arrange marriages, sell handmade goods, and share information and experiences.

Rural women are burdened with heavy workloads. They fetch all the wood and water—carrying loads weighing 44 to 55 pounds (20 to 25 kilograms) on their heads for long distances. They do all the cooking and housework and care for the children.

The widespread use of the narcotic plant qat by men in Yemen negatively affects the lives of many women and children. The men of the household spend their afternoons chewing qat and socializing. Regular users spend as much as half the family's income on qat. Some of the money goes to the government, which places a 20 percent tax on qat sales. But the government sees qat as a drain on the nation's farmland, water, and income. To set an example, President Saleh no longer chews it.

Parents usually arrange marriages for their daughters. In return, the bride's father receives money from the groom or his family. In some regions, arranged marriages are similar to business deals in which men earn great amounts of money. The government has tried to discourage this practice by limiting the amount of money men are allowed to offer for a wife. Laws also ban the marriage of girls under sixteen years of age. The average age for marriage is twenty-two for men and eighteen for women. Islam allows men to have up to four wives at a time, but most Yemeni men marry only one.

The unification of Yemen created new educational opportunities for the nation's women. More Yemeni women receive schooling and fill positions in business and education. The literacy rate, especially in the cities, is rising fast as more girls attend schools. Universities accept women students but still give men priority in admission.

CULTURAL LIFE

The religion of Islam is the most important cultural factor in Yemeni life. Almost all Yemenis are Muslim. The religion and the Arabic language give Yemenis a shared culture with Arab Muslims throughout the Middle East. However, distinct cultural practices remain strong in Yemen. The tradition of creating poems on the spot, for instance, is one way Yemenis express their values and views.

◉ Religion

The state religion of Yemen is Islam. Less than 1 percent of Yemenis follow other religions. After Israel became an independent Jewish state in 1948, most Yemeni Jews moved to Israel. Although the remaining Jewish population is small, it represents the largest non-Muslim group in the country. Small Christian and Hindu communities exist in southern Yemen. Hinduism has been the dominant religion of India since about 1500 B.C.

Islam means "submission" [to the will of Allah] in Arabic. *Allah* is the word for "God." Muslims believe that Allah gave messages to his prophet Muhammad through the angel Gabriel. The holy scriptures of the Quran contain these messages. This monotheistic religion shares roots with Jewish and Christian religions. These three major world religions arose in the same part of the world.

Muslims strive to fulfill five central duties of faith, known as the five pillars of Islam. They are: declaring faith in Allah and his prophet; praying five times daily; giving charity; fasting from sunrise to sunset during the holy month of Ramadan; and making a pilgrimage to the holy city of Mecca once in a lifetime, if possible. Friday is the holy day of the week for Muslims. Men go to the mosque to hear teachings and to pray. Women pray at home or in separate parts of the mosque.

Modesty is also an important virtue in Islam. Muslims across the world interpret the call to modesty differently. Strict traditional Muslims, for instance, believe women should cover themselves from

MENSWEAR

In the hot coastal regions, men wear a lightweight shirt and an embroidered skirt called a *futa*. A straw hat or other head covering keeps off the sun. In the colder highlands, a long shirt is worn with a jacket. Most men in the north wear belts that hold a jambiya. These curved daggers identify the wearer's clan.

Men in highland clothing perform a traditional dance in Wadi Dahr, Yemen.

head to toe when they appear in public. Some women in Yemen follow this style of dress. Some women and men, especially in big cities, dress in Western styles.

Like Christianity, Islam has split into many different branches and sects. Its two main branches are Sunni Islam and Shiite Islam. Sunnis make up the orthodox, or dominant, branch. Sunnis and Shiites differ mainly in their manner of choosing leaders. Sunnis choose leaders from among all Muslims. Shiites believe only descendants of the prophet Muhammad can be imams.

Yemen has three distinct subgroups within the two branches. These are the Shafiis, the Zaydis, and the Ismailis. About half of the country's population is Shafiis. This Sunni sect dominates southern Yemen. They make up a wealthy and powerful merchant class. One-third of Yemeni Muslims are Zaydis. This Shiite subgroup once ruled the country and still strongly influences the government. Class differences have caused divisions between the two sects. Another important difference between the Shafiis and the Zaydis lies in each sect's view of the Quran. Like most Muslims, the Shafiis believe that the Quran is the word of God as told to Muhammad. The Zaydis, however, believe the prophet Muhammad created the Quran.

Ismaili Shiites have beliefs similar to the Zaydis. They make up only about 2 percent of the population. Most Ismailis live near Manahka in the Central Highlands.

Holidays

Islamic holy days follow a lunar (moon-based) calendar, so the seasons of holidays change over time. The Islamic calendar counts years starting with Muhammad's journey from Mecca to Medina, Saudi Arabia, in 622. Muslims celebrate this journey, called the hegira, on Muharram 1, the first day of the Muslim year.

The most important Islamic holy time is the month of Ramadan. This is the month when Muhammad became Allah's prophet. Observant Muslims do not drink or eat anything between sunrise and sunset all month. The whole country slows down during the day. However, people gather for meals at night. Ramadan ends with two days of feasts and worship, called Eid al-Fitr. Muslims buy new clothes, clean their homes, and visit friends and family at this joyful time.

The other main Islamic holidays are Mouloud (Muhammad's birthday) and Eid al-Adha, or the Feast of the Sacrifice. During this three-day festival, people who can afford it have a sheep slaughtered and share the meat with the poor. The holiday comes at the end of the month of pilgrimage to Mecca, known as the *hajj*.

Secular holidays in Yemen follow the same solar calendar that Western nations normally use. New Year's Day is on January 1. The Day of National Unity on May 22 celebrates the creation of the Republic of Yemen in 1990. Revolution Day 1962 on September 26 commemorates the overthrow of the Zaydi imams in the north. Revolution Day 1967 on October 14 and Independence Day on November 30 honor the struggle against British rule in the south. Yemenis also celebrate weddings and harvests with music and dance.

ISLAMIC LAW

Besides following the Islamic way of life, Muslims in Yemen also follow Islamic law. Sharia is based on the Quran and the hadith—written collections of Muhammad's sayings and deeds. The laws forbid having sex outside marriage, drinking alcohol, gambling, and more. Punishments for breaking the laws are sometimes harsh. Islam also teaches that people should behave generously, fairly, modestly, honestly, and respectfully.

Weddings

Several days of festivities mark weddings in Yemen. Men and women celebrate separately. The legal ceremony involves signing a contract in the presence of an Islamic law official. The final day of the wedding usually occurs on Friday, the Islamic holy day. Men gather in the afternoon, while women cook the wedding feast. In the evening, the men go to the mosque to pray. On the way back, they sing and dance around the

A Yemeni woman shows off the **henna art** on her hands.

groom. He dresses in traditional clothes and carries a golden sword. Then the men enjoy the food the women have prepared. They pass incense and blessings, chew qat, recite poems, play the oud—an ancient stringed instrument that is the ancestor of the European lute—and sing songs.

In the meantime, women help the bride prepare at her home. A special body painter spends hours applying dye made from the henna plant. She traces delicate designs on the bride's hands and feet. The bride wears her best traditional jewelry.

After the feast, the men line up singing outside the groom's house. He walks past them toward his door and leaps over the doorstep. The women climb onto the roof of the groom's house. While they are waiting for the bride to arrive with her father, they make a high-pitched sound. The men continue to sing. Once the bride enters the groom's house, she becomes part of his family.

◉ Music and Dance

Music is an important part of festive occasions in Yemen, and dancing often accompanies it. Poem singers are popular and often sing at qat chews.

Music styles vary by region. In the cities, musicians play the *kabanj* (lute) and two small drums. In the Tihama, cymbals and violins accompany fast, intricate rhythms. Another traditional instrument is the one-stringed *rebaba*. In the highlands, the music is more reserved. Musicians play a double-reed pipe called a *mizmar* and beat a drum with their hands. The drummer often sings.

Ayoob Tarish Absi is one of Yemen's most respected traditional singers and musicians. He is known as Yemen's Bulbul (a songbird). Hearing villagers and farmers singing of their joys and sorrows during his childhood influenced Absi's music. Reciting the Quran as a boy taught him the rhythms of Classical Arabic. He plays the oud, and his songs convey the spiritual comfort of Islam and the singer's love of his country. He composed Yemen's national anthem.

The *jambiya* dance is Yemen's best-known dance. Men with daggers dance in a pattern of dignified turns, knee bends, steps, and hops. Ouds and rhythmical instruments mark the beat of the moves. This dance is different in each region and emphasizes loyalty among clan members. People dance the *luabah* dance in pairs at weddings or harvest celebrations. Song lyrics for this dance speak of love or religious praise. In public, men dance with men. At women's parties, women dance together. A woman and a man may dance together in private.

Literature

The most important book for Yemeni Muslims is the Quran. People have recited its prayers and stories for centuries. The nation also has a rich tradition of spoken literature. Nearly every village can trace its history and traditions through poetry and song. Local poets help to celebrate marriages or other occasions by creating verses on the spur of the moment. Traditional poetry is often broadcast on radio and television or sold as recordings. Through poetry, Yemenis discuss a wide range of topics.

Yemeni poetry takes different forms. The *zamil* is a two-line poem, often concerning politics. Its strict rules of meter and rhyme create beautiful patterns of sounds. Competing poets trade zamils they make up on the spot.

Abdullah al-Baradouni (1929–1999) is considered Yemen's most famous poet and writer. His poems call for democracy and women's rights. Besides twelve books of poetry, he published books discussing politics, folklore, costumes, and literature. His criticism of the government landed him in jail in the mid-twentieth century. Sayyid Ahmad

This sixteenth-century Persian art illustrates a **tenth-century poem about three Yemeni princesses.** To find out more about cultural life in Yemen, go to www.vgsbooks.com for links.

Amin Mashreki writes poetry against violence and people who carry out bombings. One of his poems deals with the attack on the USS *Cole*. In it, the poet asks, among other things, what the ship, the sea, and the fish have done to deserve such an attack.

Zabara (1908–2000) was an important religious leader who composed 360 poems about the history of Yemen.

Yemen's literature is little-known outside the country. Zayd Mutee Dammaj writes some of Yemen's leading fiction, some of it available translated into English. His novel *The Hostage* was published in English in 1994. Set in the former North Yemen of the imams, it tells the story of a boy from the countryside. Soldiers take him hostage to make sure his father and clan obey the ruling imam. As the boy grows into a young man, the reader sees the reality of life without personal freedom—one of the motives for the revolution against the imam.

Arts

Islam forbids images of Allah or human beings on religious paintings and sculptures. Therefore, Muslim artists developed complex geometric designs to decorate their mosques and houses. Detailed illustrations and calligraphy (decorative handwriting) beautify volumes of the Quran. Only plants, animals, and nonliving things appeared in religious paintings.

Some modern artists choose to paint portraits of people, despite Islamic tradition. The growth of a modern art movement that began in the twentieth century reflects interaction with outside cultures. Artists who studied abroad introduced different media to Yemeni art, such as oil paints, watercolors, and silk-screen prints.

In such a poor country, it is difficult for artists to make a living. Fuad al-Futaih is one of Yemen's most successful modern artists. Breaking with Yemeni tradition, he depicts the women of Yemen in bright, bold paintings. In a country where women appear in public dressed in black veils, his paintings are revolutionary. In 1993 al-Futaih founded the Modern Art Group, to encourage young artists. One such artist who won success is Mazher Nizar. He paints traditional architecture and women in watercolors. Both artists exhibit in Yemen and abroad.

Yemen's craftspeople create silver jewelry, handwoven textiles and baskets, wooden boxes, and other crafts. A special Yemeni craft is the making of curved ceremonial daggers called jambiya. Artisans inlay designs into the daggers' handles. The most valued dagger handles are made of rhinoceros horn from Africa. The National Handicrafts Training Center in Sanaa sells modern craft items. Women produce embroidered bags, purses, and jackets, and other items. This center was established to help disadvantaged women earn a living. In 2006 the government opened a newly enlarged National Museum in Sanaa.

ART VERSUS WILDLIFE

Daggers with rhinoceros-horn handles are highly prized in Yemen. In fact, Yemen's demand for rhinoceros horn is so high, it has helped drive rhinos to the brink of extinction.

jambiya

Young people play **soccer in a village near Sayun, Yemen.** All they need is a ball and an open, level place to play.

Sports

Men and boys play soccer, called football in Yemen, all over the nation. Competitive teams exist but have not yet reached world-class level. Boxing is also popular in Yemen. Boxing champion Naseem Hamid Kashmim (b. 1974) grew up in Great Britain with his Yemeni parents. Some teams play cricket, a bat-and-ball game from Great Britain. Other organized sports are rare in Yemen. Citizens and the government do not have money for sports equipment and training. Yemeni athletes compete in the Olympic games but have not yet brought home medals.

Food

Yemen's fertile land and ocean waters provide the country's main foods—bread grains, beans, rice, vegetables, lamb, goats, and fish. The diet of Yemen is simple. Bread—served warm—is the most important food. The nation counts almost thirty kinds of bread. Bakers bake some kinds of unleavened, or flat, breads in a special oven called a *tanour*. Some of the breads are pizza-sized and spongy. Diners tear the bread into pieces to scoop up hot food rather than using spoons or forks. They also dip bread into yogurt or sauces.

Breakfast is a light meal of scrambled eggs with tomatoes and bread. Breakfast may also be a bean dish called *ful*—a stew of fava, or broad beans, onions, tomatoes, and chilies, served with flat bread. Yemenis eat their main meal at midday. It typically consists of bread,

TOMATO AND CILANTRO SALAD (BANADURA SALATA B' KIZBARA)

This salad is a refreshing start to a meal. Be careful handling the chili pepper. Its juice can burn skin and eyes.

5 large ripe tomatoes

½ cup finely chopped cilantro

1 small chili pepper, such as jalapeño, seeded and finely chopped

4 tablespoons fresh lemon juice

½ teaspoon salt

¼ cup olive oil

1. Slice the tomatoes. Place in a bowl. Sprinkle the cilantro over the tomatoes.
2. In another bowl, mix the chili pepper with the lemon juice and salt. Pour in the olive oil and mix well.
3. Pour the oil dressing over the tomatoes and cilantro. Let rest 15 minutes at room temperature before serving.

Serves 6 to 8

beans, and vegetables such as tomatoes, potatoes, green beans, and cucumbers. If people can afford meat, lamb and chicken are favorites. Religious law forbids Muslims to eat pork or drink alcohol. Rice mixed with raisins and almonds may accompany meals. Thick lamb or lentil soup is a common dish. Cool yogurt soup is refreshing on hot afternoons. The national dish is a spicy stew called *salta*, served over bread or rice. It contains lamb or chicken, beans, lentils, chickpeas, and spices. Typical spices are fenugreek, cinnamon, cloves, cumin, chili, and coriander. Sometimes mint adds flavor to dishes and to the hot, sweet tea that Yemenis drink all day long.

For dessert, Yemenis enjoy sweet custard or fruits such as peaches, grapes, and figs. *Qishr* is sweet, thick coffee spiced with ginger. Yemenis make qishr by boiling powdered coffee, sugar, and ground ginger in a long-handled, Arab-style coffeepot. It is served in tiny coffee cups after meals. At festive meals, people dip sweet bread called *bint as-sahn* into butter and honey. Yemen's excellent honey is widely known. Honey from the Wadi Hadhramawt region is a special delicacy.

THE ECONOMY

Yemen is a poor country, with an average income per person of $920 yearly. This is a little less than the average for East African countries across the Red Sea and the Gulf of Aden. In comparison, the Middle East's average annual income per person is $7,500. Inflation in Yemen is very high, with prices rising about 12 percent yearly.

High oil prices around the world boost Yemen's economy. The country relies on oil for 70 percent of the government's budget. Relying on one source of income, however, makes the economy unstable. The Yemeni government would like to diversify, or develop other industries. It wants to expand agriculture, which has been the country's traditional economic mainstay. The government also seeks to develop transportation and communication systems further. These improvements would make Yemen more attractive to foreign companies and tourists, despite serious security issues.

Yemenis also rely partly on remittances, or money sent home from family members working in other countries. Large numbers of

Yemenis live and work in other countries on the Arabian Peninsula, East Africa, Indonesia, India, Great Britain, and the United States.

Before unification, both Yemens depended heavily on financial aid from other countries. The United States, Europe, and the oil-rich Arab nations helped North Yemen to build new roads, telephone lines, and hydroelectric power plants. South Yemen leaders relied on aid from Communist countries after the 1967 revolution. Unified Yemen also receives outside assistance. For instance, the World Bank, a United Nations agency, sponsors nineteen projects in Yemen. These include improving government, water, and education. The country's stance during the Persian Gulf wars was unpopular among some of Yemen's aid donors. Still, other nations see aid to Yemen as important to the entire region's stability.

Political stability in Yemen is crucial to oil producers in the region, which holds much of the world's oil. Yemen sits at the entrance to the Bab el-Mandeb Strait, linking the Red Sea to the Indian Ocean. The

British Petroleum built the original **Aden oil refinery.** The Yemeni government took control of the refinery in 1977.

strait is one of the most important shipping lanes in the world. Tankers carrying about 3 million barrels of oil per day use the lane. Disruption to shipping in the strait could force tankers from the Persian Gulf and the Gulf of Aden to travel at great cost around the southern tip of Africa.

Industry, Oil, and Mining

Industry provides 48 percent of Yemen's gross domestic product, or GDP, the value of goods and services produced in a country in a year. The industry sector includes manufacturing, mining, and construction. Oil production and refining makes up the bulk of the earnings. Yemen refines its own oil as well as oil from countries on the Persian Gulf. For decades Yemen's Middle Eastern neighbors have exported huge quantities of oil from underground fields. In the early 1980s, the two Yemens explored their territories and found deposits of oil large enough for refining and export.

North Yemen quickly developed its oil resources with the help of U.S. companies. By 1986 five oil wells were pumping near Marib, and workers had laid a pipeline from the oil fields to the Red Sea. By 1989 North Yemen was producing more than 200,000 barrels per day. South Yemen joined forces with a Soviet company in the late 1980s. But it still lacked the facilities to transport more than about 6,000 barrels daily. After the two Yemens united in 1990, a new pipeline was built. Output increased to more than 120,000 barrels per day in the territory of former South Yemen.

The government hopes to boost Yemen's oil production to 400,000 barrels per day. Officials signed contracts with foreign companies to develop this valuable resource. Yemen's oil goes mostly to Asian markets, including China, India, and Thailand.

Yemen's network of pipelines transports crude oil and natural gas to several export terminals on the coast. Yemeni production relies on private foreign companies. More than twenty foreign firms operate oil companies in the country. Yemen continues to sell licenses to companies, mostly foreign, to explore for new oil fields.

Engineers also found natural gas reserves in north central Yemen. This discovery stimulated plans for construction of a gas-processing plant, gas-fired power stations, and a factory for bottling liquefied petroleum gas.

Yemeni mines and quarries produce salt, limestone, and marble. Yemen's fish processors use some of the salt found along the Red Sea coast as a preservative for fish sent to inland markets, but most is exported. Limestone from the Tihama supplies the cement industry. Cement factories, however, do not produce enough to meet domestic needs. Miners have quarried marble in Yemen since ancient times. It remains one of the country's most important goods. Alabaster and pastel-tinted marbles are in great demand for the construction of traditional buildings throughout the country. Mining contributes less than 1 percent of industry, but companies continue to prospect for minerals in Yemen. Gold is known to exist in Yemen, and mining companies are especially interested in the possibility of new discoveries of gold.

Before the revolutions of the 1960s, lack of raw materials and facilities limited Yemen's industrial growth. Industries then included the manufacture of textiles, leather, baskets, jewelry, and glassware. These handicrafts are still money earners for Yemen.

A **Yemeni vendor's booth** in Sanaa overflows with pottery and baskets.

Read the latest news from Yemen and find information about its economy. Go to www.vgsbooks.com for links.

After unification, Yemen expanded its industrial base by building factories that make soft drinks, cigarettes, small aluminum products, and food products. Small-scale industry also produces cotton textiles and leather goods. Ship repair takes place in port cities.

The government seeks investment to develop more industry, such as fish-canning factories. In 2001 building began in Aden on a large new industrial estate. The largest project on the new site is a sugar refinery. As the country develops, it calls on its construction industry. Construction workers build new factories, roads, houses, and more.

Transportation and Communications

Yemen's poor transportation system slows the export of the country's goods. As recently as the 1980s, donkeys and camels were the main form of overland transportation. Many people still use these animals in rural regions.

Making improvements in transportation is a priority for the government. A network of 6,286 miles (10,116 km) of paved roads crosses the entire nation. The rest of the total 40,480 miles (65,146 km) of roads, tracks, and trails are unpaved. In the highlands, the rugged terrain is a major obstacle for road construction crews.

Yemen has forty-five airports, sixteen of which are paved. International flights enter Yemen through airports at Aden, Sanaa, Taizz, and Hodeida. The major airline—Yemen Airways—flies to Europe, Asia, and Africa, as well as to many cities within Yemen.

The ports of Aden and Hodeida offer access to major sea routes. Ships from many nations use the ports for refueling, repair, and a place to transfer cargo. Mukalla is an important fishing port. It is 22 miles (35 km) from Yemen's main oil export terminal. A twelve-year development plan for major modernization of Yemen's ports began in 2003. With improved roads, as well as sea and air links, Yemen has the potential to develop a profitable foreign trade.

Most Yemenis rely on television and radio for news, because many people cannot read. The ministry of information, a part of Yemen's government, strictly controls the news media, radio, television, and the press. Courts have sentenced reporters to prison for

A Yemeni lumberjack stands on his camel's load of tree trunks to demonstrate the animal's strength. Camels continue to provide transportation in rural Yemen.

articles that criticize the government. The ministry controls the printing presses and runs the official daily newspaper, *al-Thawrah*. The Republic of Yemen television station is also state run. The *Yemen Times* is a weekly English-language newspaper with a reputation for speaking freely.

Yemen created a national telecommunications system after unification. Fewer than 1 million landline telephones are in use in Yemen, but more than 1 million Yemenis use cellular phones. Only 220,000 Yemenis are Internet users.

Services and Tourism

The service sector offers public and private services rather than producing goods. It includes jobs in government, health care, education, banking, retail trade, and tourism. Yemen's government is the largest service employer. It hires medical workers, teachers,

Tour operators promote Yemen as the new frontier in adventure travel. They offer hiking trips to mountain villages and sailing voyages to isolated islands. Safari travelers in four-wheel-drive vehicles journey along old incense trading routes.

laborers, administrators, and more. Services provide 39 percent of the nation's GDP.

Yemen holds potential as a tourist destination. In contrast to the rest of the Arabian Peninsula, Yemen offers cool, green land under deep blue skies and mountain villages untouched by the modern world. However, terrorism and kidnappings reduced the number of tourists in 2000. Yemen's security efforts, with U.S. help since 2001, have reduced terrorism and made traveling in Yemen safer. About 155,000 tourists visit Yemen yearly, mostly from other Middle Eastern countries. The tourism industry adds $140 million yearly to the economy.

Agriculture and Fishing

Northwestern Yemen contains some of the most fertile land on the Arabian Peninsula. Its seacoasts provide ample fishing. As a result, the country has the potential to meet its own food needs. For this reason, agriculture, including fishing, has long been crucial to Yemen's economy. About 54 percent of the overall population make their living as farmers and fishers. Among rural people, agriculture provides 58 percent of male employment and 95 percent of female employment. Though the sector employs more than half the workforce, it provides only 13 percent of the GDP.

Most farms are small and produce only enough crops to feed families or local communities. Yemen's hot climate supports sorghum, millet, and barley. Fruits are plentiful, including citrus fruits, apricots, and pomegranates. Farmers grow cash crops to sell, such as tobacco, sesame, coffee, and cotton. In eastern Yemen—where temperatures are warmer—bananas, dates, and grapes thrive along the wadis. Plans are under way to build new irrigation systems, which will increase the variety of crops that can be planted in Yemen.

Coffee, once Yemen's most profitable export, is grown sparingly alongside qat in the highlands. Coffee growers cut terraces into the hills for coffee plants. Qat claims more acreage and makes more money than any other crop in the country. Though legal in Yemen, leaves of this plant are considered a drug and cannot be exported legally. Farmers plant qat on much of the land that once supported food crops. The increased cultivation of qat hurts Yemen's efforts to meet its own food needs.

Yemenis also breed livestock throughout the country. Herders raise sheep, goats, cattle, and camels for their milk, meat, and hides. Farmers also manage commercial chicken farms. In addition, some people keep bees and make Yemeni honey, which is highly valued for its quality and taste.

Local production of food has not kept pace with the country's growing population, and Yemen must import food. Uncertain rainfall also hampers crop growing, and Yemen relies on imports—especially of wheat.

The government places high priority on agricultural development plans. Aid from other countries funds much of these plans. Financing goes toward irrigation, dam building, and water storage systems.

The government also aims to increase fish production. One of the richest fishing areas in the world lies along Yemen's coast. Strong seasonal winds bring cool, nutrient-rich waters to the surface, causing plants and plankton to grow. As a result, a large variety of fish—such as tuna, mackerel, cod, red snapper, and lobster—feed in the area. Commercial boats, as well as small, independent fishing rigs, haul in large amounts of fish every year. Storage plants exist throughout Yemen, and canning factories operate in the coastal areas.

This **clay beehive in Bayt al-Faqih, Yemen,** is one type of hive in use there. *Baghiyyah* means "an object of desire" in Arabic. It is the name of one of Yemen's best honeys.

Three **young people from Taizz** smile for a tourist's camera.

▶ The Future

Yemen's 2004 Sanaa Declaration highlights the importance of free elections, the rule of law, a free media, rights of women, and a healthy economy. Yemen has far to go in making these values a reality. The country struggles to make progress in the face of many political, social, and environmental challenges. The economy relies too heavily on oil earnings. The government hopes to attract much-needed investment to carry out economic reforms.

The country also looks to outside aid as it attempts to improve social services such as education and health care. A high birth rate and ongoing gender inequality limit women's full participation in their nation's well-being. Water scarcity presents a crisis for Yemen. Poor water quality and sanitation damage the nation's health.

HOPE FOR THE FUTURE

Before the 2006 presidential elections, President Saleh spoke of his hopes for Yemen's peaceful future: "I hope that all political parties . . . find young leaders to compete in the elections because we have to train ourselves in the practice of peaceful succession. Our country is rich with young blood who can lead the country . . . let us transfer power peacefully among ourselves. . . ."

Security issues inside and outside Yemen threaten the nation and the larger region. In response, Yemen's government works with the United States and other nations to reduce global terrorism. It has had some success in maintaining stability among the country's different groups, and in recent years there has been little al-Qaeda activity in the country. The 2006 presidential elections demonstrated an Islamic democracy at work. Burdened with high levels of poverty and unemployment, Yemen's citizens struggle to create a brighter future.

CA. 38,000 B.C.   The first humans migrate to present-day Yemen from East Africa.

CA. 5000 B.C.   People in Yemen use flint tools and build water channels and stone dwellings.

CA. 1000 B.C.   Three kingdoms arise in Yemen: Saba (Sheba) and Qataban in the Central Highlands and Hadhramawt in eastern Yemen. The kingdoms grow wealthy from the trade of frankincense and myrrh.

CA 900 B.C.   The legendary visit of Bilqis, the queen of Sheba, to King Solomon takes place.

CA. 500 B.C.   The Sabaeans build the Marib Dam on an important wadi. The dam will last until A.D. 570.

A.D. 50   Himyarites take advantage of newly discovered sea routes and conquer south-western Arabia.

323   The Roman emperor Constantine makes Christianity the official religion of his empire, leading to the decline in the frankincense and myrrh trade.

525   The Christian king of Ethiopia seizes Yemen after the Sabaean king executes twenty thousand Christians.

575   At the Himyarites' request, forces from Persia (Iran) defeat the Ethiopians and bring Yemeni kingdoms under Persian rule.

628   The Persian governor of Yemen accepts Islam. The new religion soon spreads throughout the country.

897   Al-Rassi becomes the first imam of the Zaydi dynasty. This ruling family will last almost one thousand years.

1067   Queen Arwa inherits the Sulayhid throne.

1548   The Ottoman Turks bring most of Yemen under their control.

1636   Under the leadership of Muayyad Muhammad of the Zaydi imams, Yemen ends Ottoman Turk occupation.

1839   Forces of the British Empire seize Yemen's port, Aden.

1849   The Ottoman Turks return to Yemen and occupy the Tihama.

1905   The British and the Turks divide Yemen into Turkish-controlled northern Yemen and British-controlled southern Yemen. The Zaydis continue to resist Turkish rule.

1918   After the Turkish defeat in World War I, northern Yemen becomes fully independent of the Ottomans. Zaydi rule governs the north, while the British keep control of the south.

1949   Operation Magic Carpet airlifts most Yemeni Jews to safety in the new state of Israel.

1962   A coup overthrows the Zaydi imams and establishes a republic called the Yemen Arab Republic (YAR), known as North Yemen. Civil war breaks out between royalists, who support the imams, and republicans.

1967   The National Liberation Front (NLF) forces the British to leave Yemen and founds the People's Republic of South Yemen (renamed People's Democratic Republic of Yemen, PDRY, two years later).

1970   The republicans win the northern civil war , and North Yemen gains Saudi Arabian and European support. Tensions are high with Communist-supported South Yemen.

1979   The successful Islamic Revolution in Iran inspires Islamists around the world. Communist Soviet troops occupy Afghanistan. Yemeni troops join Afghan Muslim fighters against the occupation, which will last ten years.

1982   An American company finds oil near Marib. Continued development of an oil industry encourages the two Yemens to try to unify.

1990   On May 22, North and South Yemen officially unite as the Republic of Yemen. Iraq's invasion of Kuwait threatens the stability of the region.

1993   Artist Fuad al-Futaih founds the Modern Art Group to encourage promising young artists.

1999   An extremist group kidnaps sixteen foreign tourists. Voters in Yemen's first direct presidential elections choose Ali Abdullah Saleh.

2000   Terrorists bomb the USS *Cole* in Aden, killing seventeen sailors, and also attack the British embassy in Yemen.

2001   After the September 11 terrorist attacks on the United States, President Saleh pledges Yemen as a partner with the United States in the fight against global terrorism.

2003   U.S.-led forces invade Iraq and remove the regime of Saddam Hussein. Yemenis protest the invasion.

2004   Yemen hosts an international meeting on democracy and human rights. The government issues the Sanaa Declaration, stressing the importance of political and social freedoms. The Literacy Through Poetry project teaches women to read and write through recording their own poetry.

2005   Clashes between government forces and northern Zaydi (Shiite) rebels called the Young Believers lead to hundreds of deaths. A landslide destroys a village near Sanaa, killing more than sixty people.

2006   The newly enlarged National Museum in Sanaa opens. In September Yemenis reelect President Saleh in a landslide. Fighting in Somalia drives almost twenty-three thousand Somali refugees into Yemen.

2007   Renewed clashes between Yemen's government and the Young Believers lead to dozens of deaths.

COUNTRY NAME Republic of Yemen

AREA 203,849 square miles (527,969 sq. km)

MAIN LANDFORMS Haraz Mountains, Wadi Hadhramawt, Central Lowlands, Western Highlands

HIGHEST POINT Jabal al-Nabi Shuayb, 12,336 feet (3,760 m) above sea level

LOWEST POINT Sea level

MAJOR RIVERS No permanent rivers

ANIMALS Arabian gazelles, baboons, camels, foxes, hares, hedgehogs, honey badgers, hyenas, hyraxes, mongooses, porcupines, chameleons, cobras, geckos, vipers, butterflies, mosquitoes, mackerel, sardines, sharks, squid, Arabian woodpeckers, flamingos, lammergeiers, ravens, seagulls, weaverbirds, Yemen thrushes

CAPITAL CITY Sanaa

OTHER MAJOR CITIES Aden, Taizz, Hodeida

OFFICIAL LANGUAGE Arabic

MONETARY UNITY Yemeni rial (YR, also spelled riyal); 1 rial = 100 fils

YEMEN CURRENCY

At unification, lawmakers reorganized the new nation's currency. Yemen's banknotes, or paper money, are in denominations of YR1000, 500, 200, 100, 50, and 20. Coins are in denominations of 10, 5, and 1 rial, and 10 and 5 fils. Colorful images of Yemen's history, landscapes, and architecture adorn the banknotes.

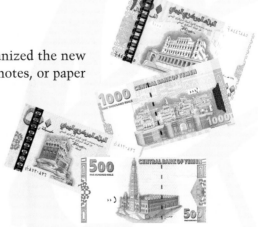

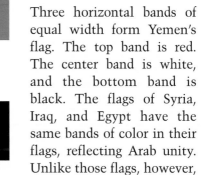

Three horizontal bands of equal width form Yemen's flag. The top band is red. The center band is white, and the bottom band is black. The flags of Syria, Iraq, and Egypt have the same bands of color in their flags, reflecting Arab unity. Unlike those flags, however, the flag of Yemen has no other decoration.

This song became the anthem of South Yemen in 1967, when it had no title. The anthem gained the title "United Republic" when North and South Yemen joined in 1990, at which time it became the anthem of the unified country. Abdullah Abdulwahab Noaman wrote the lyrics. Ayoob Tarish Absi wrote the music. The English translation of part of the anthem follows.

"United Republic"

Repeat, Oh World, my song.
Echo it over and over again.
Remember, through my joy, each martyr.
Clothe him with the shining mantles of our festival.

Repeat, Oh World, my song.
Repeat, Oh World, my song.

Oh my country, we are the sons and grandsons of your men.
We will guard all of your majesty in our hands.
Its light will be immortal on all ways,
Every rock on your mountains, every particle of your soil.

Repeat, Oh World, my song.
Repeat, Oh World, my song.

In faith and love I am part of mankind.
An Arab I am all my life.
My heart beats in tune with Yemen.
No foreigner shall dominate over Yemen.

 Visit www.vgsbooks.com for a link to a website where you can hear Yemen's national anthem.

Famous People

ABDULRAHMAN ABDULAZIZ (birthdate unknown) Yemeni athlete Abdulaziz is a long-distance runner. He won the gold medal in the Young Arab Championship Games in Damascus, Syria, in June 1998. Abdulaziz trained by himself, sometimes going without enough food to eat. The Yemeni Athletics Federation (YAF), one of the most active sports groups in Yemen, encouraged Abdulaziz. In 1999 Abdulaziz participated in the World Championship Marathon in Northern Ireland. Afterward he did not return to Yemen.

ROSA MUSTAFA ABDULKHALEQ (b. 1976) Abdulkhaleq is Yemen's first female commercial airline pilot. After getting her private flying license, she studied in Texas to gain her commercial license in 2002. Yemen's national airline hired her as a pilot. Many see her as a symbol of women's rights in Yemen and the Arab world.

AYOOB TARISH AL-ABSI (birthdate unknown) Nicknamed Yemen's Bulbul (a songbird), al-Absi composes and performs traditional Yemeni songs and music. He plays the oud, a kind of lute. Born in the countryside of al-Aboos, he credits reciting the Quran and hearing the chants of farmers and villagers as his biggest influences. Al-Absi composed the national anthem. His song "Come Back to Your Land" persuaded many Yemenis in the 1990s not to leave their homeland. His music expresses religious sentiments meant to bring peace of heart and mind. His personal favorite is his beautiful song "Jala' al-Qalb" (Clarity of the Heart).

QUEEN ARWA (d. 1138) *Malika* means "queen" in Arabic, and Queen Arwa is also known as Malika Arwa. She is one of the only women to become head of state in the Arab world after the coming of Islam. Arwa held power for almost half a century, from 1067 to her death in 1138. Another female head of an Islamic state was Arwa's mother-in-law, Queen Asma. Arwa married Asma's son al-Mukarram. After his death, Arwa ruled as a popular and capable queen from 1067 until her death in 1138. She moved her capital from Sanaa to the more secure mountain fortress of Jabala. From there, her forces were victorious in battles against enemies. She ordered new roads, religious centers, monuments, and buildings to be built.

ABDULLAH AL-BARADOUNI (1929–1999) Al-Baradouni is considered Yemen's most famous poet. He was born in the Zaraja village of al-Hadaa. When he was six years old, smallpox left him blind. He began writing poetry when he was thirteen, and in his lifetime he published twelve books of poetry. He also wrote about politics and folklore, and he taught Arabic literature. The poet valued ancient traditions, but he also spoke out for modern democracy and women's rights. The North Yemen government imprisoned al-Baradouni for his poems critical of the leaders who took power in 1962. His works are read throughout the Arab world and have been translated into many languages.

AHLAM SALEH BIN BREIK (b. 1958) Bin Breik is a doctor, based in Mukalla. She is also a professor of medicine at Hadhramawt University and a married mother of four. *Yemen Times* selected her as its Person of the Year in 2006. Bin Breik told the newspaper that she decided to study medicine when she was twelve, after she watched her younger sister die of diarrhea. Bin Breik directs the Hadhramawt society for fighting AIDS, founded in 2004.

FUAD AL-FUTAIH (b. 1948) Al-Futaih, a Yemeni artist, was born in North Yemen but grew up in Aden. Though he lived through revolutionary times, he always focused on art, theater, and literature. He studied abroad before returning to Sanaa. In 1993 al-Futaih founded the Modern Art Group to encourage young artists. One of the Arab world's most successful artists, his main subjects are Yemen's history, landscape, and women. His artistic expression of female sexuality breaks with tradition. In an interview, the artist said that he aims to create Islamic Arab art with a strong, modern personality.

MOHAMMED AL-HASSAN AL-HAMDANI (ca. 893–945) Al-Hamdani was an Islamic scholar in Yemen. He was also a poet. Scholars consider his *Geography of the Arabian Peninsula (Kiidl Jazirat ul-Arab)* an important work. Al-Hamdani also wrote about astronomy, chemistry, language, and the history of the Himyarites. Little is known about his life. He lived during the turbulent last years of the Abbasid dynasty. According to legend, he died in prison in Sanaa.

ALI ABDULLAH SALEH (b. 1942) In 1978 Saleh became the president of North Yemen in a coup. In 1990 he became the first president of unified Yemen. Saleh joined the army when he was sixteen. He rose through the ranks to become field marshal. Under his stable leadership, Yemen settled border disputes and put down civil strife in the country. Saleh's government is an important participant in the global war on terror. Though alliance with the West is not always popular, Saleh has the backing of Yemen's powerful army. Saleh won his second official term in 2006, with 77 percent of the vote.

ABDULAZIZ AL-SAQQAF (1952–1999) Al-Saqqaf founded Yemen's first and most important English-language newspaper, *Yemen Times*, in 1991. A champion of human rights, Al-Saqqaf was also a professor of economics at Sanaa University. In 1995 the *Yemen Times* won the American National Press Club's International Award for Freedom of the Press. Al-Saqqaf died after being hit by a car in 1999. In 2006 the Middle East Publishing Conference awarded their Achievement Award to al-Saqqaf's work promoting freedom of the press.

Though Yemen is a beautiful and hospitable country, the U.S. Department of State warns: "The security threat level remains high due to terrorist activities. . . ." For updated travel warnings, check http://travel.state.gov/travel/cis_pa_tw/tw/tw_936.html.

HARAZ MOUNTAINS The Haraz Mountains on Yemen's western edge are a hiker's delight. Well-used walking trails link lush green mountaintops and pass through timeless villages of mud and stone houses.

MAKHA Ruins of old Makha remind visitors of the ancient glory of this city, when it was Yemen's most important trading port. The most important feature of Makha is the five-hundred-year-old al-Shadeli Mosque. About 58 miles (93 km) from the city of Taizz, Makha overlooks the Red Sea. Nearby, tourists can visit beautiful beaches surrounded with palm and coconut trees.

MARIB The ruins of the ancient Sabaean site are considered the cradle of civilization in southern Arabia. Located on the edge of the Empty Quarter, the town was once the capital of a great kingdom based on the incense and spice trade. Visitors can tour remains of the ancient dam.

SANAA Ancient walls with eight gates enclose the medina, also called the Old City, in the center of Yemen's capital. UNESCO, a United Nations agency, declared the entire Old City a World Heritage Site. Visitors may feel as if they are part of the old tales of the *Arabian Nights*. About 2,500 years old, the capital features ancient architecture and winding alleys. Famous mud-brick "tower houses" rise up to eight stories high.

SHAHARAH A famous bridge leads to this remote hilltop village set in beautiful mountain scenery in northern Yemen. This village served as a fortress of resistance to the Ottomans in the 1600s. Residents sculpted the mountainside, creating a deep basin to hold runoff from rain. People meet and chat on the basin's many steps.

SHIBAM High in the foothills of Wadi Hadhramawt, this walled village dates from the A.D. 100s. It was built on the ruins of the ancient city of Hadhramawt. Its grand mosque dates from the 900s. People come to Shibam's colorful Friday market. Travelers call it the Manhattan of the Desert due to its mud-brick houses. Neighbors can visit across skywalks that connect one rooftop to another. UNESCO placed Shibam on its Human Heritage list. The nearby ancient town of Tarim has 365 mosques, one for each day of the year.

SOCOTRA (OR SUQUTRA) ISLAND This island is a naturalist's paradise, lying 210 miles (338 km) off Yemen's coast. It is home to unique plants, such as the cucumber tree. Sea turtles nest on its unspoiled beaches. Scuba divers explore spectacular reefs.

Arabic: the official language of Yemen. Classical Arabic is the language of the Quran.

desertification: the process of drylands turning into barren desert, caused by a combination of factors, including drought and overuse of land

gross domestic product (GDP): the value of goods and services produced in a country in a year. Gross national product (GNP) also counts foreign income.

hadith: a collection of the sayings and actions of the prophet Muhammad

imam: an Islamic title for a leader, especially a leader of prayers. The imams of the Zaydi dynasty were both spiritual and political leaders from 897 until 1962.

Islam: a worldwide religion founded through the prophet Muhammad in the seventh century. Allah's messages to Muhammad are in the Quran.

Islamist: a person who believes sharia should govern a country

jambiya: a curved, ceremonial dagger, worn by Yemeni men in a belt around their waists. The designs of the daggers show the wearer's clan membership.

literacy: the ability to read and write basic sentences

mafraj: Arabic for "room with a view"—the top floor of a house, used as a living room for guests and qat chews

medina: the old, walled section of an Arab city, which a modern city grows around. In Sanaa the Old City is the medina of the modern capital city.

mosques: Islamic places of public worship and prayer

Muslims: followers of Islam. *Muslim* means "one who submits [to the will of God]" in Arabic.

PDRY: People's Democratic Republic of Yemen, or South Yemen, formed in 1967 after the British withdrew. On May 22, 1990, it merged with the YAR.

qahwa: Arabic for "coffee." Westerners called Yemen's superior coffee *mocha.*

qat: (also spelled *khat*) a mildly narcotic plant whose leaves many adults in Yemen chew for their stimulating effect

Quran: the holy book of Islam. In Arabic, *al-Quran* means "the recitation." Sunni Muslims believe these scriptures are the word of God.

sharia: Islamic teaching and law based on the Quran and the hadith. Sharia regulates matters such as marriage, divorce, inheritance, and some crimes.

sheikh (or shaikh): "elder" in Arabic, a title used for a leader. In Yemen a clan chief or village leader is called sheikh.

souk: a marketplace with specific areas for different goods and trades, such as carpets or jewelry making. Souks also sell modern goods such as DVDs.

wadis: riverbeds that run with water during the rainy season

YAR: the Yemen Arab Republic, or North Yemen, began in 1962 with the revolution that overthrew the last Zaydi imam. In 1990 it merged with the PDRY.

Selected Bibliography

BBC News.
http://www.bbc.co.uk/ **(February 2007).**
The World Edition of the BBC (British Broadcasting Corporation) News is updated throughout the day, every day. The BBC provides a country profile of Yemen at http://news.bbc.co.uk/go/pr/fr/-/2/hi/middle_east/country_profiles/784383.stm.

British Yemeni Society.
http://www.al-bab.com/bys/about.htm **(January 2007).**
The British-Yemeni Society promotes friendship and expanded public knowledge about Yemen, its history, geography, economy, and culture. Its website offers articles by members with expertise on wide-ranging topics.

Caton, Steven C. *Yemen Chronicle: An Anthropology of War and Mediation.* **New York: Hill and Wang, 2005.**
Professor Caton, director of Harvard University's Center for Middle Eastern Studies, first went to Yemen in 1979 as a student. This book is a memoir of his three-year stay and his 2001 return to Yemen. Caton researches water management in Yemen. A 2006 *Yemen Times* interview, "Harvard Professor Discusses Yemen from 1979 to 2006," by Brock L. Bevan, can be found online at http://yementimes.com/article.shtml?i=990&p=report&a=1.

Central Intelligence Agency (CIA). "Yemen." *The World Factbook.* **2006.**
https://www.cia.gov/cia/publications/factbook/geos/ym.html **(November 2006).**
This CIA website provides facts and figures on Yemen's geography, people, government, economy, communications, transportation, military, and more.

Downey, Tom. "Yemen: An Arabian Oasis for the Intrepid." *New York Times.* **December 10, 2006.**
The *New York Times* names Yemen the Adventure Destination of the Year in this article. The author examines tourists' options to explore this beautiful land.

Dresch, Paul. *A History of Modern Yemen.* **Cambridge, UK: Cambridge University Press, 2000.**
Anthropologist and scholar of Yemen, author Dresch relates an in-depth story of Yemen's modern history, from the Ottoman and British division of Yemen through the union and following civil strife. He uses poetry, local quotations, and personal experience to present a fascinating slice of a little-known country.

Energy Information Administration. "Yemen Country Analysis."
http://www.eia.doe.gov/emeu/cabs/Yemen/Background.html **(January 2007).**
This site is one of the most complete sources of energy statistics on the Internet. It offers information about energy production and use in Yemen and other countries of the world. The site includes links and a kids' section.

Gordon, Frances Linzee, Anthony Ham, Virginia Maxwell, and Jenny Walker. *Arabian Peninsula.* **Hawthorn, AUS: Lonely Planet , 2004.**
Besides political and geographic information about Yemen, this book offers special chapters on religion and language shared by the nations of the Arabian Peninsula. Lonely Planet's website about Yemen can be found at http://www.lonelyplanet.com/worldguide/destinations/middle-east/yemen/.

Gordon, Matthew. *Islam.* **Rev. ed. New York: Facts On File, 2001.**
This book, part of the World Religions series, provides an overview of Islam. It discusses the religion's history, basic beliefs, and the modern Islamic world. Illustrations and sidebars accompany the informative text.

Hämäläinen, Pertti. *Yemen.* **Hawthorn, AUS: Lonely Planet, 1999.**
A guide for the adventurous traveler, this book offers an overview of Yemen's long history, awesome natural beauty, and rich cultural heritage. Maps, color photographs, and entertaining sidebars round out helpful travel information.

Hoyland, Robert G. *Arabia and the Arabs: From the Bronze Age to the Coming of Islam.* **London and New York: Routledge, 2001.**
Using a wide range of sources, including art and literature, this book provides a survey of ancient Arabia, including Yemen. Illustrations include the Marib Dam, coins, statues, and maps.

Mackintosh-Smith, Tim. *Yemen: The Unknown Arabia.* **Woodstock, NY: Overlook Press, 2000.**
Illustrated with etchings by Martin Yeoman, this book gives a full picture of Yemen. Part travel journal, part history book, *Yemen* is filled with descriptions written by an Arabic scholar who has lived in the country since 1982.

Mernissi, Fatima. *The Forgotten Queens of Islam.* **Minneapolis: University of Minnesota Press, 1993.**
A Moroccan professor of sociology, Mernissi investigates the role of women in the Arab world. She challenges conventional beliefs about Islam and women's history in this presentation of women who governed Muslim states. A long section on Yemen looks closely at the queens Asma and Arwa and their times.

The Middle East and North Africa, 2006. **London: Routledge, 2006.**
This book is part of the annual Europa Regional Surveys of the World series. Its long section on Yemen covers the country's geography, culture, and recent history.

Population Reference Bureau.
http://www.prb.org (January 2007).
The PRB provides annual, in-depth demographics on Yemen's population. Its data sheets include statistics relating to health, environment, education, employment, family planning, and more.

Sallah, Tijan M. "Women of Color: An Artist's Obsession Breaks Yemeni Tradition." *Worldview Magazine,* **Summer 1999.**
http://www.worldviewmagazine.com/issues/summer1999/topstory.html (November 2006).
This article features the Yemeni artist Fuad al-Futaih.

U.S. Department of State, Bureau of Near Eastern Affairs. *Background Note: Yemen.* **January 2006.**
http://www.state.gov/r/pa/ei/bgn/35836.htm (November 2006).
The background notes of the U.S. State Department supply a profile of Yemen's people, history, government, political conditions, and economy.

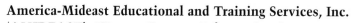

America-Mideast Educational and Training Services, Inc. (AMIDEAST). "Yemen Country Information."
http://www.amideast.org/offices/yemen/country_info.htm
AMIDEAST, headquartered in Washington, D.C., is a nongovernmental organization that works to strengthen mutual understanding and cooperation between Americans and the peoples of the Middle East. This site offers information focusing on Yemen.

Arabnet
http://www.arab.net
This useful site from Saudi Arabia collects news and articles about the entire Arab world. It also offers links to sites about specific countries, including Yemen.

Behnke, Alison, and Vartkes Ehramjian. *Cooking the Middle Eastern Way*. Minneapolis: Lerner Publishing Co., 2005.
Yemen shares many dishes with other Middle Eastern countries. Lamb is the most commonly used meat, and locally grown beans, rice, dates, and nuts are popular ingredients. Many countries in the region have similar cuisines. Each nation also has its own specialties, leading to a diverse blend of dishes.

Dammaj, Zayd Mutee. *The Hostage*. Brooklyn: Interlink Books, 1994.
Set in North Yemen before the revolution against the rule of the imams, this novel is written by Yemen's best-known fiction writer. It relates the story of a boy taken hostage in order to guarantee his father's loyalty to the imam. The young man is kept as a servant in a palace. There he comes to know the women of the household, who are trapped without freedom too. He eventually rebels and regains his independence.

Hansen, Eric. *Motoring with Mohammed: Journeys to Yemen and the Red Sea*. Boston: Houghton Mifflin, 1991.
Traveler, adventurer, and writer Eric Hansen first found himself in Yemen when he was shipwrecked in the Red Sea on his way to Greece. He returned ten years later to get back his notebooks, which he had buried to keep safe and then left behind. He also wanted to explore the country that had captured his imagination. This book is the story of Hansen's travels around Yemen with his guide Mohammed and others. He meets all kinds of people, listens to stories, chews qat, and eventually gets his journals back.

Hestler, Anna. *Yemen*. New York: Marshall Cavendish, 1999.
Part of the Cultures of the World series for younger readers, this volume offers colorful photos, maps, and charts. Chapters describe the history, geography, economy, language, and culture of Yemen.

Jelloun, Tahar Ben. *Islam Explained*. New York: The New Press, 2004.
This is an excellent book for anyone who wants to learn about Islam in modern times. The book offers a clear introduction to the history and main beliefs of Islam. Presented in a question-and-answer format, the Muslim author responds to his young daughter's questions about being Muslim. The book also defines words often heard in the news, such as *terrorist*, *jihad*, and *fundamentalist*.

Maréchaux, Pascal, and Maria Maréchaux. *Impressions of Yemen.* **New York: Flammarion, 1997.**
The authors are photographers who have traveled in Yemen for twenty years. They captured the brilliant colors and designs of the country's architecture in this lush book of photographs. Images of clothing, makeup, and interiors further illustrate the life of Yemen's people.

The Middle East Network Information Center. "Yemen."
http://menic.utexas.edu/Countries_and_Regions/Yemen/
This site is a public service of the Center for Middle Eastern Studies at the University of Texas at Austin. It offers links to information on Yemen's news, maps, education, arts, science, and more.

Quin, Mary. *Kidnapped in Yemen: One Woman's Amazing Escape from Captivity.* **Guilford, CT: Lyons Press, 2005.**
Mary Quin was one of sixteen travelers to Yemen kidnapped in 1999 by extremists. In this book, she tells the fascinating personal story of her journey back to Yemen as she attempts to understand the full picture behind the events that left four of her fellow travelers dead.

Sallis, Eva. *The City of Sealions.* **Crows Nest, AUS: Allen & Unwin, 2002.**
This novel follows Lian, a young Australian woman living and studying Arabic in Sanaa. The reader sees daily life in Yemen through Lian's eyes as she falls in love and struggles with being a stranger in a strange land.

Searight, Sarah. *Yemen: Land and People.* **London: Pallas Athene, 2002.**
The beauty and antiquity of Yemen are well presented in this book filled with color photographs by Jane Taylor. The text aims to introduce newcomers to the history, people, and scenery of the remarkable country.

vgsbooks.com
http://www.vgsbooks.com
Visit vgsbooks.com, the home page of the Visual Geography Series®, which is updated regularly. You can get linked to all sorts of useful online information, including geographical, historical, demographic, cultural, and economic websites. The vgsbooks.com site is a great resource for late-breaking news and statistics.

Yemen Gateway.
http://www.al-bab.com/yemen/Default.htm
Bab means "gate" in Arabic, and al-Bab.com is a gateway to the Arab world. This is its home page for Yemen. It offers links to basic information on Yemen, including the latest news, local time, and weather. It also provides several useful links to selected websites such as the Yemeni embassy in London.

Yemen Times
http://yementimes.com/index.shtml
The first issue of Yemen's "most widely read" English-language newspaper appeared in 1991. Online, the *Yemen Times* offers local news, top international news, and opinion pieces. Features cover culture, health, and environmental issues.

Index

Abdulaziz, Abdulrahman, 70
Abdulkhaleq, Rosa Mustafa, 70
Absi, Ayoob Tarish al-, 50–56, 69, 70
Afghanistan, 32, 34, 35
AIDS, 40, 71
al-Qaeda, 32, 34, 35, 36, 65
animals, 4, 12, 14, 24, 60, 63;
    camels, 4, 20–21, 22, 61; honey
    badgers, 14
Arabic, 40–41
Arabian Peninsula, 7, 8
Arab countries, 7, 22, 29, 44, 46. *See
    also* Middle East
architecture, 17, 18, 19, 42–43, 53
arts and crafts, 44, 50, 52, 53, 60, 71

Bab el-Mandeb Strait, 8, 15, 23,
    57–58
Baid, Ali Salim al-, 33, 34
Baradouni, Abdullah al-, 51–52, 71
Bible, 4, 16, 22
Bin Breik, Ahlam Saleh, 71
Bin Laden, Osama, 32, 34, 35
Bush, George W., 35, 36

censorship, 61
cities, 11, 16–19, 38, 72; Aden, 7, 12,
    18, 28, 33, 35, 60; Hodeida, 15, 19,
    60; Makha, 27, 72; Marib, 19, 21,
    24, 72, 80; Sanaa, 16–18, 33, 37,
    72; Taizz, 19, 80
clothing, 34, 44, 45, 48
coffee, 13, 27, 55, 62
Communism, 30, 31, 57
counterterrorism, 35, 36, 65

daggers (*jambiya*), 48, 51, 53
Dammaj, Zayd Mutee, 52
democracy, 7, 34, 36, 37, 64
desert, 9, 16, 20; Empty Quarter, 11,
    12–13
dragon blood tree, 13

East Africa, 7, 8, 37, 56. *See also*
    Somalia
economy, 7, 16–19, 33, 34, 56–64;
    agriculture, 15, 56, 63–64; industry
    and manufacturing, 58–60; mining,
    15, 58, 59; oil and gas, 5, 7, 15, 19,
    29, 56, 58–59; qat, 15, 45, 62;

remittances, 33–34, 56–57;
    services, 61–62; tourism, 63, 72;
    trade, 18, 60; transportation, 61
education, 7, 25, 40–41, 45
environment, 14, 53
ethnic groups, 18, 43

farms and farming, 5, 9, 11, 38,
    62–63; qat, 13, 62
fishing, 15, 19, 63
food, 49, 54–55, 62; honey, 55, 63
foreign relations, 33–34, 36, 37, 57
Futaih, Fuad al-, 53, 71

Great Britain, 34; in Yemen, 5, 27,
    30, 35
gross domestic product (GDP), 56,
    58, 62

Hamdani, Mohammed al-Hassan al-,
    71
Haraz Mountains, 11, 68, 72
health, 39–40, 71
henna, 50
history, 4–5, 7; British rule, 5, 27, 30;
    early kingdoms, 4, 19, 20–23,
    25–26, 42; foreign invasions,
    26–28; North-South split, 5, 27–31;
    Ottoman rule, 5, 26–28; rise of
    Islam, 4–5, 24–25; Saba (Sheba), 4,
    22; unification, 5, 7, 32–33
holidays, 47
honey, 55, 63
housing, 42–43. *See also* architecture
human development index, 39
human rights, 36
Hussein, Saddam, 36

imams, 25
incense plants, 4, 13, 22, 23
Iran, 32
Iraq, 7, 22, 25, 33, 40; war in, 33–34,
    36
Islam, 4–5, 7, 24–25, 41, 45, 46–49;
    art and, 53; laws of, 24–25, 32, 37,
    45, 49, 55; politics and, 28, 29, 32,
    34; sects of, 24–25, 37, 48
Islamist militants, 7, 31–32, 34, 35,
    36
islands, 8; Socotra, 8, 13, 16, 26, 72

Israel, 7, 22, 29, 34, 35, 40

Kuwait, 33

languages, 4 , 25, 41–42, 46
lifestyles: rural, 7, 38, 44, 62; urban, 16, 17, 38, 48
literacy, 7, 41, 45, 61
literature, 7, 40, 51–52, 71; poetry, 7, 40, 41, 46, 50, 71; proverbs, 51

Marib dam, 21, 24, 80
markets (souks), 17, 72, 80
Mashreki, Amin, 52
media, 42, 51, 61, 71
Middle East, 15, 38, 44, 46, 56; tensions in, 7, 33–34, 35, 37, 65
mosques, 17, 24, 72, 80
mountains and volcanoes, 9, 11, 12, 72
music and dance, 48, 49–51, 70

natural resources, 15
North Yemen, 5, 27–28, 29, 32, 57, 58; civil war, 29–30, 31–32, 36; unifies with South, 5–6, 32–33

poetry, 7, 40, 41, 46, 50, 71
political parties, 41
proverbs, 51

qat, 13, 15, 45, 62, 80
queens: Arwa, 26, 70; Asma, 71; of Sheba, 4, 22
Quran, 22, 24, 25, 40, 41, 47, 48, 51

rainfall, 9, 12
Ramadan, 47, 49
recipe, 55
recreation, 13, 45
refugees, 7, 29, 34, 37, 43
religion, 23–25, 46–49; ancient, 21, 22; Christianity, 23, 46; Judaism, 23, 29, 46. See also Islam
roads, 7, 18, 61
Roman Empire, 4, 23

Saleh, Ali Abdullah, 7, 32, 33, 34, 35, 36, 45, 64, 71
sanitation, 40

Saudi Arabia, 8, 29, 31, 33, 35, 44
sharia (Islamic law), 24–25, 32, 37, 45, 49, 55
ships and shipping, 5, 7, 15, 18, 23, 35, 58, 60
social structures, 43–44
Somalia, 7, 8, 34, 37, 43
South Yemen, 5, 27, 28, 30, 31, 57, 58; civil war, 32; unifies with North, 5–6, 32–33
Soviet Union, 29, 31, 32, 34
sports, 54, 70
Suez Canal, 27

terrorism, 7, 32, 34–37, 63, 65; kidnappings, 34; September 11, 35; USS *Cole*, 7, 35, 52
trade, historic, 4, 20–21, 22–23, 26, 72; modern, 18, 60
transportation, 18, 60

United Nations, 18, 29, 39, 43, 57, 72
United States, 7, 28, 33; relations with Yemen, 34, 35, 36, 65

wadis, 9, 11–12, 15, 28, 43, 48, 55, 62, 80
wars: civil wars, 29–30, 31–32, 34; Persian Gulf, 33, 36, 57; World War I, 29
water, 40; bodies of, 5, 8, 15, 27, 57–58; shortage of, 7, 9, 15, 16, 65
weddings, 45, 49–50, 51
women, 34, 38, 40, 41, 44–45, 47, 53, 64, 70, 71; rulers, 22, 26, 70

Yahya, 28, 80
Yemen: boundaries, size, and location, 4, 7, 8; climate, 12; currency, 68; flag, 69; flora and fauna, 13–14, 68; government, 37; maps, 6, 10; names, 4, 7, 12, 22; national anthem, 69; population, 4, 16, 38; topography, 7, 8–9, 11–12
Young Believers, 36, 37

Zaydis, 25, 28, 29, 31, 48

Captions for photos appearing on cover and chapter openers:

Cover: Imam Yahya, king of North Lebanon from 1926 until his death in 1948, built this five-story rock palace in the 1930s as a summer residence. It is a landmark in the valley of Wadi Dahr, 12 miles (19 km) northwest of the capital city of Sanaa.

pp. 4–5 People buy and sell livestock at this traditional open-air market in a remote part of Yemen.

pp. 8–9 These fields of qat lie near Amran, Yemen.

pp. 20–21 Ruins of a dam near Marib date back to about 500 B.C.

pp. 38–39 Yemeni young people in Zabib grin happily for the camera.

pp. 46–47 In Taizz, Yemen, the whitewashed domes of the Al-Ashrafiya Mosque stand out.

pp. 56–57 Donkeys carry a family group returning from the market in Hodeida, Yemen.

Photo Acknowledgments

The images in this book are used with the permission of: © Cory Langley, pp. 4-5, 16-17, 38–39, 45, 50, 53, 56–57, 59, 61, 64; © XNR Productions, pp. 6, 10; © Helene Rogers/Art Directors, pp. 8–9, 43; © Tibor Bognar/Art Directors, p. 11; © Tomas van Houtryve/Panos Pictures, p. 13; © Francois Savigny/naturepl.com, p. 14; © Khaled Fazaa/AFP/Getty Images, pp. 18, 58; © A.A.M. Van der Heyden/Independent Picture Service, pp. 20–21, 46–47; © North Wind Picture Archives, p. 22; © Robert Harding Picture Library Ltd./Alamy, p. 23; The Art Archive/Marine Museum Lisbon/Dagli Orti, p. 26; AP Photo, p. 29; © Terry Fincher/Hulton Archive/Getty Images, p. 30; © Thomas Hartwell/Time & Life Pictures/Getty Images, p. 33; © Lyle G. Becker/AFP/Getty Images, p. 35; © Wolfgang Kaehler, 2008—www.wkaehlerphoto.com, pp. 41, 54; © Cris Bouroncle/AFP/Getty Images, p. 48; The Art Archive/Musée Condé Chantilly/Dagli Orti, p. 52; © F. Jack Johnson/Alamy, p. 63; Audrius Tomonis—www.banknotes.com, p. 68 (all); © Laura Westlund/Independent Picture Service, p. 69.

Front Cover: © Cris Bouroncle/AFP/Getty Images. Back Cover: NASA/JSC.